Redeeming Shakespeare's Words

REDEEMING

SHAKESPEARE'S WORDS

BY PAUL A. JORGENSEN

UNIVERSITY OF CALIFORNIA PRESS

Berkeley and Los Angeles

1962

UNIVERSITY OF CALIFORNIA PRESS
Berkeley and Los Angeles

CAMBRIDGE UNIVERSITY PRESS
London, England

© 1962 *by The Regents of the University of California*

Library of Congress Catalog Card Number: 62-9940

DESIGNED BY RITA CARROLL

PRINTED IN THE UNITED STATES OF AMERICA

To my family

PREFACE

In recent Shakespeare scholarship, imagery in the plays has been studied in an attempt to find how motifs were, consciously or not, expressed through dominant images or image clusters. But words, even more than images, are the vehicles with which the poet-playwright worked; and yet there has been little attempt to study these in the contexts of the plays and the literature of the time.

Most of the following essays are devoted to the fullest possible explication of words that are either thematic or significant in certain plays. I have tried to choose key words, to find their Renaissance connotation, and to see how this connotation was utilized by Shakespeare in his dramatic message. All of these steps are necessary if we are to redeem Shakespeare's words for the modern reader.

I place the essay on *"Honesty in Othello"* first, because it best illustrates the importance of finding the exact meaning of a crucial word and also because it most fully displays the type of research that is necessary if one would place a pivotal Shakespearian word in its rightful context. To discover what *honesty* connoted to an audience of 1604, I found myself studying not only the morality play (in which the word was used in its most popular and fundamental sense) but also treatises, including the Diogenes literature, in which Elizabethans read of the problem of finding an honest man in a troop of knaves. Here, as in most of the other essays, I have had to seek the word in its "live" state, as C. S. Lewis has done in his recent *Studies in Words* (Cambridge, England, 1960). This has entailed reading in many fields not obviously related to literature. For the essay on "Much Ado About Nothing," I had to read works ranging from ephemeral mock encomia to sturdy theological treatises on doctrines of creation (dealing both with creation of man and with creation of literary works). For the essay on Pistol, my major sources were military textbooks now found only in rare book collections. And for my essay on " 'Redeeming time' in *Henry IV*," I found myself hopelessly committed to reading sermons.

Not all of the essays follow the same pattern; not because I willed it that way but because it was unpredictable where the context of a word might lie. In "Hamlet's World of Words," for example, I was forced to deduce the context of the word mainly from an intent reading of the play itself, though I do finally suggest clues toward finding the fuller connotation, notably in other plays of Shakespeare. In viewing the word primarily in the context of the play, I have been helped by the precedent set by Professor Robert B. Heilman, notably in his *Magic in the Web: Action and Language in Othello* (Lexington, Kentucky, 1956). Not all of the essays are of equal substance. Though Pistol is an interesting word, it does not dominate its play as does *honesty,* and I have accordingly given it a very short explication.

Perhaps the range in procedures will not be entirely meaningless. Shakespeare did not, I am sure, deliberately choose a body of writings to form the context for an important word. Had he been more conscientious in this respect, my task would have been simpler and the method of the book more uniform. Because, like Coleridge's, his habits of reading were apt to be flexible and unpredictable, I have had to depend upon extensive browsing and sheer luck to track him to his contexts. The varying approaches of the following essays reflect, I trust, some of the hopeful doggedness that must be used by future investigators who will undoubtedly succeed in bringing out the full connotation of other important words.

From more scholars than I can name here, I have received much assistance during the years I have given to this book. Professor Willard Farnham, whom his students will always know as a distinguished teacher as well as scholar, taught me to study Shakespeare; and he has ever since remained a source of kindly counsel and encouragement to me. To my colleagues Professors Hugh G. Dick, William Matthews, and James E. Phillips I have been constantly indebted for wise advice. Geoffrey Ashton did everything that an editor could do to make the manuscript clear and consistent. As with most students, my indebtedness extends beyond individuals to foundations. A grant from the John Simon Guggenheim Memorial Foundation permitted me to carry on these studies; and I am especially grateful to the Henry E. Huntington Library. Without the splendid resources of this hospitable institution and the stimulating scholars who visit it, I could not have written this book.

P. A. J.

CONTENTS

He ha's a strange forc't appetite to Learning, and
to atchieve it brings nothing but patience and a body.
His Studie is not great but continuall, and consists
much in the sitting up till after Midnight in a rug-gowne,
and a Night cap to the vanquishing perhaps of some sixe lines:
yet what hee ha's, he ha's perfect, for he reads it so long
to understand it till he gets it without Booke.

John Earle's "A Plodding Student"
from *Micro-cosmographie* (1628)

CHAPTER I

Honesty in OTHELLO

Assuredly one of the most spectacular touches in
Shakespeare's mature workmanship is the lavish use
of *honest* and *honesty* in *Othello,* with frequent application to the villain of the play. Critics have rightly
questioned the artistic propriety of such usage. Julian
Abernethy noticed that his soul was "tormented by
the endless repetition of the word 'honest,' " and
"Honest Iago" proved to be an "irritating phrase,"
which "distracts attention from the main issues of the
plot with which the mind should be absorbed, jars
upon the nerves like a discord in music, transgresses the
rules of dramatic consistency, and detracts from the
dignity of tragic drama." [1] If Shakespeare was merely

[1] " 'Honest Iago,' " *The Sewanee Review,* XXX (1922), 336.
Neilson and Hill take a more resigned attitude: "How so wicked
a man could acquire and maintain a name for honesty it is futile

playing, though brilliantly and ironically, with the word, Abernethy's reaction presents a serious indictment of the drama. Even William Empson's attempt to assign a meaning to most of the many uses of the word does little to change one's impression that the play's merit is mainly one of surface brilliance and virtuosity.[2]

There is undoubtedly, as Empson contends, considerable flux in Shakespeare's use of *honest,* and there is the inevitable yielding to the pun. Of all Elizabethan words, *honest* had possibly the most bewildering instability of meaning. Shakespeare could not pass such an opportunity by. But led by the conviction that he would not cheapen powerful tragedy by excessive word play, I have sought in Elizabethan usage some predominant connotation of *honest* that would relate language to theme in *Othello.* This is to be found, I believe, in the widespread and urgent Elizabethan problem: How may one know the honest man from the knave?[3]

---

to wonder, but everybody believes in 'honest Iago,' . . ." (*The Complete Plays and Poems of William Shakespeare,* eds. W. A. Neilson and C. J. Hill [Cambridge, Mass.: Riverside Press, 1942], p. 1095). [Unless otherwise stated, all Shakespeare references are to this Neilson and Hill edition.] See also W. R. Hallet, "Honest Iago," *The Fortnightly Review,* LXXIX (1903), 257–286.

[2] "The Best Policy," *Shakespeare Survey* (London, n.d.), pp. 5–21. Reprinted as "Honest in *Othello*" in *The Structure of Complex Words* (London, 1952), pp. 218–249.

[3] Probably the most nearly definite usage of *honest* or *honest*

This problem received its most popular expression in the drama. Lines that state the basic predicament are found as early as 1565, in Edwards' *Damon and Pithias:*

> In a troop of honest men some knaves may stand,
>   ye know,
> Such as by stealth creep in under the colour of
>   honesty,
> Which sort under that cloak do all kinds of villainy.[4]

This reference is specifically to the informer-courtier Carisophus whom the speaker, Stephano, has detected and beaten as a knave. When Stephano agrees to stop the beating if Carisophus will pledge secrecy, the knavish courtier promises to say nothing, "as I am an honest man"—precisely the oath taken by Iago (II.iii.266). Stephano muses upon the irony of trusting "such a false knave upon his honesty." [5] But we shall find that perhaps the commonest disguise for the knave is an oath involving his honesty. Surprisingly enough, few characters in the Elizabethan drama were able to penetrate the disguise.

---

man was in its habitual antithesis to knave. Cf. Wilson's *The Pedlar's Prophecy* (1595), sig. A 4: "I can discerne an honest man from a knave"; and Heywood's *Apology for Actors* (1612): "This plays an honest man, and that a knave."

[4] *Early English Dramatists,* ed. J. H. Farmer (London, 1906), p. 46.

[5] *Ibid.,* p. 45.

One of the most obvious victims of this deceit is the character Simplicity in Robert Wilson's morality, *The Three Ladies of London,* a comparatively late example (1589) of this kind of play in its pure form. Herein a Vice, Dissimulation, whose favorite oaths are "by my honesty" and "of my honesty," [6] poses as "a right honest man," but smirkingly confides in soliloquy that his "party-colour'd head" should reveal that his "honesty is fled." [7] Only Simplicity is gulled, seeking the Vice's acquaintance, "for I love honest company." [8] Finally, even this guileless character recognizes the motley beard and exclaims his disillusionment: ". . . thou art Dissimulation: / And hast thou got an honest man's coat to 'semble this fashion?" [9]

Probably the most influential dramatic exploitation of the honest-man-and-knave confusion occurs in a semi-morality comedy, *A Knack to Know a Knave* (1594). This features the character Honesty, a personified abstraction, who, unlike Simplicity, is gifted with a knack for detecting knaves and offers his professional services to King Edgar. Although astute, however, he is a somewhat clownish personage, simple

[6] In Robert Dodsley, *A Select Collection of Old English Plays* (4th ed.; London, 1874–1876), VI, 283, 311. A second edition of this play was required in 1592.

[7] *Ibid.,* pp. 251–252.

[8] *Ibid.,* p. 253.

[9] *Ibid.,* p. 257. For an interesting study of the development of the morality Vice, with its culmination in *Othello,* see Bernard Spivack, *Shakespeare and the Allegory of Evil* (New York: Columbia, 1958).

in the sense of being unsophisticated. Honesty is successful in exposing and flagellating several knaves of
the kind typically presented as being injurious to a
kingdom: courtier, priest, conycatcher, and farmer.
These scoundrels all enjoy a reputation for honesty.
The farmer, for example, is called "an honest man"
and is praised for his "honest mind." The courtier
calls him an "honest friend" and introduces him to
the King as "honest fellow," later referring to him
again as his "honest friend." [10] Not unreasonably,
Honesty is moved to exclaim: "See how he can use my
name and not me." [11] Such generous usage makes the
word extremely confusing, but not meaningless. The
author did not intend each application to have specific
meaning. Rather, the epithet *honest* becomes merely a
method of disguise for the knave, a disguise as conventional as the respectable dress of courtier or priest.

The vogue of this play is partially indicated by the
prompt appearance of a comedy by the principal rival
company of playwrights,[12] this with a different method
and emphasis, but with a title revealing the popular
theme: *A Knack to Know an Honest Man* (1596).
The problem of the earlier play had been the unmask-
ing of knaves, of whom there had been no scarcity.
Here, instead, is presented the more thorny problem

---

[10] Tudor Facsimile Texts, vol. 75, sigs. D 4ᵛ-E 3.
[11] *Ibid.,* sig. E 1.
[12] See R. B. Sharpe, *The Real War of the Theaters* (Boston, 1935), p. 22.

of finding honest men. Sempronio, converted from
vice, devotes his later life to teaching his friends the
wickedness of the world and the way to identify honesty. At the end of the play, Sempronio makes a long
speech delineating an honest man, a speech resembling
those of the many similar Characters who were soon
to appear as representatives of the type.[13] Its require-
ments for honesty are so general (as is usually the
case) that it apparently points merely to virtue as
opposed to vice. The special magic for identifying the
honest man presumably resides in Sempronio person-
ally, for he confesses:

> Oh how I should tire both tong, thought, and pen,
> To scan out knaves from perfect honest men:
> Point where I list, if so my finger light
> On honestie, I sweare I point aright.[14]

His audience seems satisfied by his method, for the
Duke affirms:

> The worlde shall praise thee, in whose life began,
> The perfect knacke to knowe an honest man.[15]

Most of the plays considered have had characteristics
of the morality kind of drama, and it is likely that any

---

[13] Cf. Nicholas Breton's "The Honest Man," *The Good and
the Bad* (1616); Joseph Hall's "The Honest Man," *Characters
of Virtues* (1608); and John Earle's "An Ordinary Honest
Man," *Micro-cosmographie* (1628).

[14] Malone Society Reprints (London, 1910), ll. 1797–1800.

[15] *Ibid.*, ll. 1804–1805.

treatment of the honesty-knave problem would show evidence of the morality-play heritage, particularly in personified abstractions. Honesty, as a matter of fact, is often personified in later usage.[16] And several early seventeenth-century plays such as *The Honest Lawyer* and *The Honest Man's Fortune* carry in their title roles vestiges of the morality-play tradition. Moreover, Shakespeare as a playwright would probably be influenced strongly by dramatic literature, especially by such a work as *A Knack to Know a Knave,* which has been thought to be a possession of his company.

But to appreciate the widespread nature of the honesty-knave problem, it is well to consider briefly its importance in nondramatic literature. In his Elizabethan revival, Diogenes the Cynic appealed to the satirical spirit of the time as he searched for an honest man or scourged knaves. It is as a knave-lasher that he appears in Thomas Lodge's *Catheros. Diogenes in his Singularitie* (1591). Samuel Rowlands was apparently influenced by both Lodge's book and *A Knack to Know a Knave* in his tract *Diogenes Lanthorne* (1607). The pessimistic nature of this work is shown in the verses that form part of its running title:

Athens I seeke for honest men;
But I shal finde them God knows when.

---

[16] Cf. a work contemporaneous with *Othello,* Barnaby Rich's *The Fruites of Long Experience* (1604), p. 58; also *The Winter's Tale* IV.iv.606.

Ile search the Citie, where if I can see
One honest man; he shal goe with me.[17]

Diogenes grows weary of "seeking honest men in
knaves skins," finally assuming that all honest men have
been banished from the city. He spends his melancholy
time excoriating various knaves like "Bribery, taken
for an honest substantiall grave Cittizen." But even
this professional knave-hunter is victimized, and all he
has for his pains is *"A knack to knowe a Knave,"*
clearly an allusion to the popular play.[18]

Thus did the Elizabethan Diogenes burn his lantern
in vain. But important though he was as a symbol, there
are significant works of similar temper in which the famous cynic does not appear. One above all others bears
most curiously upon Othello's tragedy; perhaps no
other work could so vigorously and specifically have
warned the Moor against his fate. This book, published
in 1596, bears in its title one source of its inspiration:
*The Triall of true Friendship; or perfit mirror, whereby
to discerne a trustie friend from a flattering Parasite.
Otherwise, a knacke to know a knave from an honest
man: By a perfit mirrour of both: Soothly to say:
Trie ere you trust; Beleeve no man rashly.*[19]

In this chastening work the quest for honesty is im-

---

[17] *The Complete Works of Samuel Rowlands* (Glasgow,
1880), Vol. I.
    [18] *Ibid.*, pp. 5, 10. Cf. Rowlands' *A Paire of Spy-Knaves*
(1620?), p. 2.
    [19] The author is still unidentified except for the initials M.B.

portant chiefly as it relates to fidelity in friendship. The author, though admitting one's need for friends "into whom he may transport his affections, repose his secrets, and commit his enterprises," is emphatic in prescribing "the greatest paines and carefull industry" in finding these friends, especially in an age when "every rusticall companion & illiterate pesant can represent like a looking-glass what mans qualitie and conditions he wil." [20] Do not, the reader is warned, believe "that such a one is an honest man, because thou never foundest him otherwise: for Proteus can turne himselfe into more shapes than one." [21] Do not confuse seeming with being: "every man is not as he seems to be, the arrant knave is often taken for the honester man . . . , for men judge onely by the outward appearance and protestations of men." [22] Nothing is overlooked in the cynical examination:

> Doth he say he is thy brother: yet see thou mistrust him, doth he tel thee of his honest behaviour and vertuous life? yet se thou mistrust him, hast thou found in him some properties of an honest man, and

According to the Henry E. Huntington Library *S.T.C.*, copies exist only in the British Museum and the Bodleian. I have used a photostatic reproduction of the Bodleian copy. Present-day ignorance of this work is indicated by its absence from L. J. Mills's thorough study, *One Soul in Bodies Twain. Friendship in Tudor Literature and Stuart Drama* (Bloomington, Ind., 1937).

[20] *Triall,* sig. B 1ᵛ.
[21] *Ibid.,* sig. B 3.
[22] *Ibid.,* sig. C 2.

unfained frend: yet take some more time of trial and
watch him never the less narrowly in the meane
while: for . . . none knoweth whether hee shalbe
like himselfe to morrow or no.[23]

Only a reader fresh from the experience of *Othello* is
likely to study these coldhearted directions with sober
approval. But probably only Iago and Othello himself
would agree with this cynic's conclusion: that a man
hurt by trusting another "is to bee counted a very asse,
if hee should blame him that hath deceived him, when
there is none to be blamed but himselfe and his owne
foolishnes." [24]

The *Triall of true Friendship* is exceptional principally in the rigor of its attitude. Other works ac-
quainted Elizabethans with the need for caution in
an age wherein, as Hamlet saw it, "to be honest, as
this world goes, is to be one man pick'd out of ten
thousand." [25] It is not unlikely that Hamlet's wariness
and detachment, his slowness in accepting the honesty

[23] *Ibid.*, sig. E 2.
[24] *Ibid.* Cicero may have influenced this work; cf. John Har-
rington's *The Book of Freendeship of Marcus Tullie Cicero*
(London, 1562), p. 42. Cicero, however, lacks the bitterness of
the English author and does not deride the victim of false friendship.
[25] Cf. Henry Chettle's *Kind-Harts Dreame* (1592) (London:
Percy Society, 1841), p. 45; Barnaby Rich's *The Honestie of
This Age* (1614) (London: Percy Society, 1844), pp. 12, 14.
Shakespeare's disillusioned Timon was scarcely more cautious
than Hamlet in affirming his steward to be "Thou singly honest
man" (*Timon of Athens* IV.iii.530). Nor was he more caustic

of the Ghost, the great pains whereby he succeeds in
finding one "just" man—Horatio—and his merciless
examination of Rosencrantz and Guildenstern—his
very characteristics that have afforded most perplexity
to later critics of the play—may have been precisely
what Shakespeare found most commendable in him.[26]
To the theatergoer of 1604, Othello's tragedy may
well, to a large extent, have seemed that of a man who
lacked the vital ability to discriminate true friend from
false, honest man from knave. Such, certainly, is the
way a leading authority appraises the Moor's tragic
potentialities:

> The Moor is of a free and open nature
> That thinks men honest that but seem to be so.
>   (I.iii.405)

Strictly speaking, of course, Othello thinks a very
special individual to be honest: one who is more skill-

---

than the fashion of the age recommended when he greeted the
hypocritical Poet and Painter: "Have I once liv'd to see two
honest men?" (V.i.59), repeating the expression *honest* or *honest
men* eight times, like the flicking of a whip, in scornful application
to these knaves.

[26] Fulke Greville singled out Sir Philip Sidney's fastidiously
discriminating spirit for special praise: ". . . he piercing into
men's counsels and ends, not by their words, oathes, or complements, all barren in that age, but by fathoming their hearts
and powers, by their deeds and found no wisedom where he
found no courage, nor courage without wisdome, nor either

fully garbed in honest apparel and more securely disguised behind the label "honest" than Dissimulation,
the motley-bearded Vice of *The Three Ladies of London.*

But Iago's disguise does not stop with the usual
Vice's accoutrements. That would have been a tame
role, unworthy both of a gifted villain and of a formidable victim. The full daring and complexity of
Iago's machinations can be appreciated only if we see
in him, from beginning to denouement, the knave-hunt-
ing abilities and profession of the morality Honesty.
It is thus, most probably, that many Elizabethans would
have viewed so professionally honest a creature, both
clownish and astute, as Iago.

Such, at any rate, seems to be Othello's opinion of
his ensign. He values him as a discriminating student
of human types:

> This fellow 's of exceeding honesty,
> And knows all qualities, with a learn'd spirit,
> Of human dealings.
>
> (III.iii.258)

He also recognizes Iago as one inclined to scourge vice:

without honesty and truth" (*The Life of the Renowned Sr.
Philip Sidney* [1652], in *The Works in Verse and Prose Com-
plete of the Right Honourable Fulke Greville, Lord Brooke,* ed.
A. B. Grosart [Blackburn, England: The Fuller Worthies'
Library, 1870], IV. 39–40).

An honest man he is, and hates the slime
That sticks on filthy deeds.

(V.ii.148)

Iago himself is careful, like Honesty, to proclaim his critical nature. He tells Othello: "I confess, it is my nature's plague / To spy into abuses" (III.iii.146). And he confesses to Desdemona: "For I am nothing if not critical" (II.i.120).

But Iago's reputation does not depend upon skillful use of a label. His renown for honesty, which is often acknowledged to be one of the weaknesses of the play, takes on a more specific and credible meaning when we see him enacting, not simply claiming, the role of Honesty. During his first appearance on the stage, Iago is active in this role, instructing Roderigo concerning certain knaves to be found in the army:

> You shall mark
> Many a duteous and knee-crooking knave
> That, doting on his own obsequious bondage,
> Wears out his time, much like his master's ass,
> For naught but provender, and when he's old, cashier'd.
> Whip me such honest knaves.

(I.i.44)

The last line in particular suggests his professional function of flagellating knaves; and the phrase "hon-

est knaves," meant as a caustic reference to the conventional disguise of respectability, is uttered with
scornful emphasis on *honest,* to show that he, Iago,
is not deceived.

Later, again with Roderigo as audience, Iago flagel-
lates Cassio as a "slipper and subtle knave":

> a knave very voluble; no further conscionable than
> in putting on the mere form of civil and humane
> seeming, for the better compassing of his salt and
> most hidden loose affection? . . . a slipper and
> subtle knave, a finder of occasion, that has an eye
> can stamp and counterfeit advantages, though true
> advantage never present itself; a devilish knave. Be-
> sides, the knave is handsome, young, and hath all
> those requisites in him that folly and green minds
> look after; a pestilent complete knave.
>
> (II.i.241)

This is the scathing utterance of plain-faring Honesty
who distrusts the glib and smooth.[27] In similar vein,
Iago admonishes Othello about the knaves who
boast of amorous conquests (IV.i.25). Again, he is
prompted by Montano to notify his general of Cassio's
addiction to liquor: "It were an honest action to say /
So to the Moor" (II.iii.146). He rises to heights of
moral indignation when he points to the courtesan
Bianca as a probable agent in the stabbing of Cassio:

---

[27] Cf. *A Knack to Know a Knave,* sig. A 3.

Behold her well; I pray you, look upon her.
Do you see, gentlemen? Nay, guiltiness will speak,
Though tongues were out of use.

(V.i.108)

And he sternly refuses himself sympathy with Cassio's
plight, referring to it as "the fruits of whoring"
(V.i.116).

These segments of the play are of course generally
subordinate to a major enterprise. Iago's masterwork
as Honesty is his proving to Othello that Cassio and
Desdemona are only seeming-honest. In the overt part
of this business he resorts, as did the morality character in uncloaking scoundrels before the King,[28] to
expertly staged stratagems—the handkerchief and the
overheard conversation. But more subtle and deva-
stating is his behavior in the famous "temptation
scene," where he seems merely to rely on his reputation
for insight in such matters. Here he gives Othello the
impression that, while believing Cassio dishonest, he
is trying to suppress his knowledge. Othello asks him:

Is he not honest?
Iago. Honest, my lord?
Othello. Honest? Ay, honest.

(III.iii.103)

By contracting and pursing his brow, Iago betrays
what he apparently knows only too well. Nor does he

[28] Cf. *Knave,* sigs. C 3ᵛ-D 2.

give Othello greater ease when he lets slip from him the conventional expression of knave-honesty literature: "Men should be what they seem" (III.iii.127).

It is later in the same scene that Iago most clearly reveals the professional nature of the assistance he is giving Othello. The Moor has rebelled in rage against the onslaught of jealousy, and threateningly demands decisive proof. Iago must now make his status perfectly plain, and he eloquently does so:

> God buy you: take mine Office. Oh wretched Foole,
> That lov'st to make thine Honesty, a Vice!
> Oh monstrous world! Take note, take note (O
>   World)
> To be direct and honest, is not safe.[29]

The "Office" here might easily be mistaken by modern readers for Iago's military rank; almost certainly Iago meant his function as Honesty. He protests, in effect, that Othello would make of him not the virtue that he is, but the morality Vice. The effect of Iago's bold stroke is to chasten Othello; he should not rebuke his helper for being what he is—Honesty. "Nay, stay," he says, "thou should'st be honest." But Iago still pretends resentment:

---

[29] The above reading, that of the First Folio (as reproduced in the New Variorum edition, III.iii.432), is suggestive in its use of capitals. *Honesty* in this episode is consistently capitalized —evidence, at least, that the lack of capitals in modern editions of the play should not preclude reference to the famous personification Honesty, or its equivalent.

I should be wise; for Honestie's a Foole,
And looses that it workes for.[30]

Finally, though still coy, Iago agrees to continue the work:

I do not like the Office.
But sith I am entred in this cause so farre
(Prick'd too't by foolish Honesty, and Love)
I will go on.[31]

Thus we have Iago devotedly in the service of Othello, seeking to prove to the less discerning Moor that his trusted friend and lieutenant is not the honest man he seems. Iago himself is of course the "pestilent complete knave" of the play.[32] What complicates his role in the drama is not simply, as has been supposed, that he is a villain posing as an honest man. The irony goes one fold deeper. Iago is a knave posing as Honesty, a hunter of knaves. Hence the effect of Emilia's words, uttered though they are in ignorance of her husband's guilt:

[30] Cf. *The Winter's Tale* (IV.iv.606) : "Ha, ha! what a fool Honesty is!"; Barnaby Rich, *The Fruites of Long Experience* (1604), p. 59: "Honestie, that is of a reprehending humour . . . , shal begge his bread"; and *The Plain-Dealer* (1716; ed. 1713), Prologue: "I only Act a Part, like none of you, / And yet, you'll say, it is a Fool's Part too: / An honest Man, who like you, never winks / At Faults."

[31] *Othello* (New Variorum ed.) III.iii.470.

[32] He secretly acknowledges his real nature several times, as when in exploring his future courses he remarks (II.i.321): "Knavery's plain face is never seen till us'd."

The Moor's abus'd by some most villanous knave,
Some base notorious knave, some scurvy fellow.
O heavens, that such companions thou'dst unfold,
And put in every honest hand a whip
To lash the rascals naked through the world
Even from the east to th' west!

(IV.ii.139)

Iago is startled by this speech, for he finds himself
in it in double capacity: as the "most villanous knave,"
the "base notorious knave," and as the "honest hand"
bearing a whip in the service of Othello.

The play of *Othello* must, then, have represented
a provocative study in a subject of current interest,
with a special connotation added by the popular drama
A Knack to Know a Knave. Two of the major con-
cerns of the play relate to the subject: Iago industri-
ously engaged in revealing the dishonesty of Cassio
and others, and Othello led to ruin because he "thinks
men honest that but seem to be so." Viewed thus, the
tragedy loses much of the cheaper irony attributed
to it.[33] For the Elizabethan audience, the abundant
use and misuse of the word *honest* would have been
expected in a play dealing with honesty—real and
counterfeit. For this audience, the most striking irony
would have been also the most basic to plot design:

[33] I except here the perceptive study by Robert B. Heilman
in *Magic in the Web: Action and Language in Othello* (Lexington, Kentucky, 1956).

the curious reversal of appropriate roles wherein the
hero, who should (like Hamlet) have been most alert
for knavery in a world impoverished of honest men,
abandons his office of discrimination to a knave disguised as Honesty.

CHAPTER II

Much Ado About *Nothing*

It is generally agreed that certain words must have given Shakespeare considerably more pleasure than they give us today. The *honesty* game in *Othello,* for example, may now impress us as a cleverness unworthy of the tragic stature of the play. As I have suggested, however, Shakespeare was attempting in *Othello* a serious dramatic use of a popular literary situation in which knaves, with scarcely more disguise than the label *honest* endlessly repeated, pose successfully as honest men. The word *nothing* presents an interesting parallel, for not only did its iteration stem from popular genres, but serious writers were using it for purposes other than verbal ingenuity. And there were further similarities. Like *honesty,* the word had developed nuances just closely enough related to one another to prevent easy distinction. In its combination of one covert meaning with several overt and respectable meanings—enough to make its use permissible, but never securely so—Shakespeare must have recognized one of his favorite opportunities. The fate of both words in modern exegesis also promises to be comparable. So enlightening, one fears, has been professorial clarification of the occasional pun on *honesty,* that many students have left the classroom believing that whenever Shakespeare said "honest" he meant "chaste." Less likely to emanate from classrooms, but not for that reason the less persuasive, are the conclusions of Thomas Pyles's scholarly study of "Ophelia's 'Nothing,' " wherein he rescues the word (if not Ophelia) from a moderately respectable oblivion for a distinguished place in the "venereal vernacular of the day." [1] Without meaning to sully what Professor Pyles rightly considers the "beautiful clarity" of his findings, I should like to restore some of the larger web of meaning that lay behind Shakespeare's remarkable insistence on the word.

"Can you make no use of nothing, nuncle?" asks Lear's Fool (I.iv.143). The query strikes deeper into the King's impending tragedy than we at first realize. Certainly Lear's confident reply— "Why, no, boy, nothing can be made out of nothing"—would have struck original audiences as seriously, even ironically, wrong. In its pagan doctrine his reply opposed a vital

[1] *Modern Language Notes,* XLIV (1949), 322–323.

Christian tenet; it contradicted, in several other senses, the highly potential nature of the word and idea as demonstrated elsewhere by Shakespeare and his contemporaries; it had been underlined by a previous dialogue (I.i.89–92) in which, after Lear and Cordelia exchange emphatic *nothing*'s, the King warns her, "Nothing can come of nothing"; and it is ironically echoed by the Fool's later pronouncement upon Lear himself: "Now thou art an O without a figure. I am better than thou art now; I am a fool, thou art nothing" (I.iv.211).

The audience that thus witnessed, in one sense, much growing tragically from nothing, and, in another, kings becoming things of nothing, had been familiarized with the pattern not only by De Contemptu philosophy but by two other well-known bodies of writing. The first consisted of theological treatises affirming the original nothingness surrounding creation and the essential nothingness of all temporal things. The second was part of the literary tradition that produced mock encomia like Erasmus' *The Praise of Folly*. Both shared the purpose of defending the importance of nothingness.

Indeed, out of context it is sometimes hard to distinguish one type from the other. The theological treatises were of course marked by solemnity of purpose, for they were attempting to refute the doctrine that the Church could not allow to stand unrefuted: creation out of matter, with its implicit dualism.[2] But as the discussion thus far has inadvertently demonstrated, no solemnity of idea could control so treacherous a vocabulary as the subject was fated to contend with. Witness Sir Philip Sidney's attempt to translate with dignity De Mornay's proof from creation *ex nihilo* that God exists:

> It followeth therefore that it is a power from without us which hath brought us out of Not beeing into beeing. . . . For otherwise, from out of that nothing which we were (If I may so tearme it,) we shoulde never have come to anything at all. Now betweene nothing and something, (How little so ever that something can bee) there is an infinite space.[3]

And this was the fate of philosophical poets like Sir John Davies, John Davies of Hereford, and Fulke Greville who concentrated upon the second half of the paradox: that temporal life and matter are essentially

[2] For the theological significance of creation *ex nihilo,* see C. M. Walsh, *The Doctrine of Creation* (London, 1910).

[3] *A Worke Concerning the Trewnesse of Christian Religion* (1592), p. 4. See Henry Cuffe's ingenious attempt to explain "A making something of nothing" in *The Differences of the Ages of Mans Life* (1607) pp. 26–29. Christian works on creation typically devote an early section to this vexing matter, as does Joshua Sylvester's *Bartas. His Devine Weekes* (1605) in "The First Day of the First Weeke."

nothing. Davies of Hereford, for example, in proving the insubstantiality of life, creates little more than a jingle of *thing*'s and *nothing*'s:

> What! in the World, where all things are so rife,
> Is naught but Nothing to the same agreeing?
> And, beeing scarse suppos'd: then it is
> To Nothing next, or Nothing's like to this.[4]

The nonreligious writers gladly availed themselves of the theological argumentation, since it gave valuable support to their encomia; but their special contribution is usually revealed in verbal mazes just a little worse than accidental; for, despite a superficial concern with the ideas involved, their real interest was to make, verbally, as much as possible out of nothing.

Although there were Italian and Latin antecedents,[5]

---

[4] *Wittes Pilgrimage,* in *The Complete Works of John Davies of Hereford,* ed. A. B. Grosart (Edinburgh, 1878), II, 44. For an attempt to refute the idea that since "god created all things of nothing, therefore shall all things returne againe unto nothing," see Godfrey Goodman, *The Fall of Man* (1616), p. 19; also the discussion of this subject in Victor Harris, *All Coherence Gone* (Chicago, 1949).

[5] See Jean Passerat's *Nihil* (1567), and Francisco Copetta's *Capitolo nel quale si lodano le Noncovelle* (*ca.* 1548). The genre, still not extinct, persevered only meagerly during the Augustan period. Henry Fielding, in *An Essay on Nothing* (*Complete Works,* ed. W. E. Henley [London, 1902], XIV, 309), could cite as one who "dared to write on this subject" only "a hardy wit in the reign of Charles II" (doubtless referring to Rochester's "Upon Nothing").

the first English tract of this trifling sort was *The Prayse of Nothing* (1585), doubtfully attributed to Sir Edward Dyer.[6] This prose treatise not only claims for Nothing the distinction of being the origin and end of everything, but speculates upon how much better most things would be if Nothing had caused or influenced them. This exploitation of the word's ambiguity, especially when it is used as the subject of a sentence, is better illustrated in an anonymous ballad, apparently inspired by the tract and bearing the same title:

Nothing was first, and shall be last,
    for nothing holds for ever,
And nothing ever yet scap't death,
    so can't the longest liver:
Nothing's so Immortall, nothing can,
From crosses ever keepe a man,
Nothing can live, when the world is gone,
    for all shall come to nothing.[7]

William Lisle's poem *Nothing for a New-Yeares gift* (1603) likewise uses the word, as in its title, in both a positive and a negative sense. And in a manner remi-

[6] In "The Authorship of *The Prayse of Nothing*", *The Library,* 4th ser., XII (1932), 322–331, R. M. Sargent proposes Edward Daunce instead of Dyer.

[7] *The Praise of Nothing* (n.d.) [Huntington Library *S.T.C.* no. 20185], second stanza. I have used a microfilm of the British Museum copy.

niscent of the Queen's premonition in *Richard II,*
Lisle pays tribute to the creative pains that come from
meditating on the subject:

> Excess of studie in a traunce denies
> My ravisht soule her Angel-winged flight:
> Strugling with *Nothing* thus my bodie lies
> Panting for breath, depriv'd of sences might.
> At length recovered by this pleasant slumber,
> The straunge effects from Nothing, thus I
> wonder.[8]

Obviously the only limitation upon this type of writing is the patience of the reader, for it is an easy matter
to dilute sense with so large a proportion of nonsense
that the mind refuses to follow. Trusting indeed
would be the "Courteous and gentle Reader" who,
having survived Nicholas Breton's prefatory address
to him, attempts a serious reading of the ensuing discourse upon the various kinds of nothing. Breton's
address begins as follows:

> Reade no further than you like: . . . . If there be
> nothing that likes you, my luck is nought: in nothing
> there can be no great thing, yet something may bee
> founde, though nothing to any great purpose. Well,
> there are divers Nothings, which you shall reade
> further off. . . . Now, though I will wish you looke

[8] Second stanza; reprinted in *Fugitive Tracts, Second Series*
(London, 1875), no pagination.

for no mervailous, or worthy thing, yet shall you finde something; though in effect (as it were) nothing, yet in conceit a pretie thing to passe away the time withal. Well, if you stande content with this Nothing, it may be ere long, I will send you something, more to your likeing: till when, I wish you nothing but well.[9]

Here, indeed, is much ado about nothing. The achievement of such writing is well expressed in two concluding lines from the anonymous ballad "A Song made of Nothing":

Here you see something of nothing is made,
For of the word "nothing" something is said.[10]

To some extent, and especially in his early works, Shakespeare's interest in the word lay in this type of rhetorical chicanery. But just as the nondramatic encomiasts often combined a modicum of sense with the more obvious intent of clever iteration, so Shakespeare frequently has an idea beyond mere verbal play within his earliest Nothing jingles. When, in Sonnet 136, he says:

[9] "The Scholler and the Souldiour," in *The Wil of Wit* (1597), sig. F 4. I have used the unique copy of this edition in the Huntington Library.
[10] Roxburghe Collection, 372, 373. Printed in *The Roxburghe Ballads* (Hertford, England, 1874), II, 484.

For nothing hold me, so it please thee hold
That nothing me, a something sweet to thee.

he is making the challenge equivalent, in terms of love,
to the other types of creativity from nothing. A similar
challenge is basic to a virtuoso passage in *A Midsummer-Night's Dream* (V.i.77–89). To Philostrate's dep-
recation of the artisans' play as "nothing, nothing
in the world," and Hippolyta's insistence, "He says
they can do nothing in this kind," Theseus replies,
"The kinder we, to give them thanks for nothing."
Again, in *Much Ado About Nothing* (IV.i.269), both
Beatrice and Benedick, in their exchange of *thing*'s and
nothing's, resort to the screen of nonsense for a tenta-
tive advancement of a serious meaning:

> *Bene.* I do love nothing the world so well as you.
> Is not that strange?
> *Beat.* As strange as the thing I know not. It were
> as possible for me to say I lov'd nothing so well as
> you: but believe me not; and yet I lie not. I confess
> nothing, nor I deny nothing.

At the same time, they manage a deft indirectness by
putting *nothing* into a syntax where the other person
may choose either its negative or its positive meaning.
And in still another sense,[11] inaudible let us hope to

[11] Editors have apparently overlooked the parallel between
this dialogue and the broadside ballad beginning: "Fain would

the speakers if not to the audience, the passage might reward the combined insights of Professors Partridge and Pyles, the two most sensitive students of Shakespearian bawdry.

Shakespeare, in fact, almost always surpasses other performers in this word game in the number—nearing proportions Empsonian—of satisfactory readings he supplies. It is seldom that one of the word's appearances in a Nothing cluster is without two or more possible interpretations. No fewer than two older meanings, for example, enrich the second *nothing* in Falstaff's remark about Pistol: "Nay, an 'a do nothing but speak nothing, 'a shall be nothing here" (*2 Henry IV* II.iv.207). One meaning was *negation,* in the sense of idleness or lack of import. With this denotation in mind, Alonso reproves Gonzalo, who has been talking about his ideal commonwealth (*The Tempest* II.i. 171): "Prithee no more; thou dost talk nothing to me" —which remark, of course, gets Gonzalo fully launched on the subject. He had talked of nothing, he declares, to entertain the others, whose lungs are so nimble "that they always use to laugh at nothing." In this usage *nothing* may connote not only empty talk but the word itself, as it appeared in the idle entertainment

---

I have a prettie thing, / to give unto my Ladie: / I name no thing, nor I meane no thing, / but as pretie a thing as may bee" (in Clement Robinson's *A Handefull of Pleasant Delites,* 1584, ed. A. Kershaw [London, 1926], pp. 95–97).

of the popular encomia. In its second meaning, Falstaff's *nothing* has the same force as *naughtiness* in its original sense.[12] Christian monism encouraged the explanation of evil as mere negation. So Sir John Davies explains it in *Nosce Teipsum:*

> And then the Soule, being first from nothing brought,
>   When Gods grace failes her, doth to nothing fall;
>   And this *declining pronenesse unto nought,*
> Is even that sinne that we are borne withall.[13]

To these denotations and contexts, with their nuances too numerous to describe here, must be added the unrelated meanings made possible by *nothing*'s exceptional vulnerability to the pun. Affording a passable rhyme with *doting,* as in the twentieth sonnet, *nothing* invited confusion with *note,* another fertile word. "A Song Made of Nothing" might not suggest a quibble if there were not other examples to prove that the play upon *musical noting* was far from infrequent. Shakespeare's Autolycus uses the word to describe both the vacuity and the technique of a song: "No hearing, no feeling,

---

[12] For other examples of this privative usage of *nothing,* see *Othello* III.iii.432 and IV.i.9.

[13] *The Poems of Sir John Davies, Reproduced in Facsimile* (New York, 1941), p. 148. More elaborately, De Mornay cites as the cause of evil, "the verie nothing it self; that is to wit, that God almightie, to shew us that he hath made all of nothing, hath left a certeine inclination in his Creatures, whereby they tend naturally to nothing, that is to saye, to change and corruption" (p. 23).

but my sir's song, and admiring the nothing of it" (*The Winter's Tale* IV.iv.623). Stephano looks forward to having his "music for nothing" (*The Tempest* III.ii. 154). More doubtful, and with a primary meaning closer to "absence of sense," is Laertes' description of Ophelia's singing: "This nothing's more than matter" (*Hamlet* IV.v.174)—and here one rules out only with reluctance a punning allusion to the obscenity of the mad ditties.[14] More clearly in a musical context is the climactic appearance of the word in the involved passage on noting from *Much Ado About Nothing*:

> *Pedro.* Or, if thou wilt hold longer argument,
> Do it in notes.
>   *Balth.* Note this before my notes;
> There's not a note of mine that's worth the noting.
>   *Pedro.* Why, these are very crotchets that he
>   speaks;
> Note, notes, forsooth, and nothing.
>
> (II.iii.55)

Shakespeare's more thoughtful concern with the traditional Nothing forms may best be approached through the special slant that these apparently gave

[14] Nevertheless, a good case for suspecting puns even in situations of tension is made by M. H. Mahood, "The Fatal Cleopatra: Shakespeare and the Pun," *Essays in Criticism,* I (1951), 198; reprinted in her *Shakespeare's Wordplay* (London, 1957), chap. i. And compare Laertes' verbal cleverness on a still more trying occasion: "Too much of water hast thou, poor Ophelia, / And therefore I forbid my tears" (IV.vii.186).

to his expression of De Contemptu philosophy. Treatises on Nothing commonly divide the subject into such categories as life, time, beauty, and honor. Thus Breton's discourse contains a long monologue proving, by logical steps, that military honor belongs to the type of Nothing called "the nothing durable" (sig. G 2^v):

> An other Honour is gotten by valiancie, and that is in the Warre, whereby the Captaine winneth the Armes, that (he and) his posteritie . . . do honourably beare: yet for all this, well considered, it is nothing, for that it is not certaine: for that in Warres to day is got, that to morrow is lost: to day he gets an Ensigne, that to morrow looseth his owne Armes. . . . Hee may be accused and attainted, that never did amisse. . . . Then this Honour, I see likewise is the nothing, that is the nothing durable.

Written, if not printed, well before the penning of Falstaff's disquisition, this monologue may have come to Shakespeare's attention—in fact, the "W.S." who wrote the commendatory verses may be, as Grosart thinks possible, the dramatist.[15] Again, Macbeth's "signifying nothing," with which he closes his discourse on time and life, may have had a specific ring, now lost, to audiences accustomed to the many formal disquisitions whose equations ended with *nothing*.

[15] See A. B. Grosart's edition of Breton's *Works* (Edinburgh, 1879), I, liv.

Although in these instances Shakespeare does not depend upon the emphasis of iteration any more than do several other writers in the genre, there are many serious passages in which he does. Thus, Leontes' protest against believing his jealousy to be insubstantial is clamorous with the word:

> Is this nothing?
> Why, then the world and all that's in 't is nothing;
> The covering sky is nothing; Bohemia nothing;
> My wife is nothing; nor nothing have these nothings,
> If this be nothing.
> (*The Winter's Tale* I.ii.292)

But here, since Leontes is distraught, Shakespeare uses for valid purposes of characterization the pointless cleverness of the nondramatic writers. Furthermore, Leontes' distraction is not only expressed but aggravated by his meditating on the idea of nothingness. In like manner the "inward soul" of the rhetorically frantic Queen Isabella trembles with "nothing":

> As, though on thinking on no thought I think,
> Makes me with heavy nothing faint and shrink.
> (*Richard II* II.ii.31)

The Queen's fearful thought of nonbeing contrasts effectively with her husband's eager acceptance of it. Richard finds a pleasure, typically verbal, in dramatizing the ritual of a king becoming a thing of nothing.

He prefaces this aspect of his deposition with "for I must nothing be," and concludes it: "Make me, that nothing have, with nothing griev'd" (IV.i.201). And he privately reënacts the scene—with the same verbal play—in the episode before his death, where after being "unking'd," he straightway becomes "nothing." "But whate'er I be," he concludes,

> Nor I nor any man that but man is,
> With nothing shall be pleas'd, till he be eas'd
> With being nothing.
>
> (V.v.38)

The solacing power of Nothing, as Richard ingeniously interprets it, was a staple of the mock encomia, which rely upon ambiguity by comparing the harmlessness of Nothing with the misery occasioned by things. The prose *Prayse of Nothing* is written so that "we may more apparently perceive the good effects which come of nothing, as of the least, or no enimie of life, by whose societie many evils depart." [16] It is appropriate that the dying Timon should find no more positive words for the hereafter than the formula of the mock encomia:

> My long sickness
> Of health and living now begins to mend,
> And nothing brings me all things.
>
> (*Timon of Athens* V.i.189)

[16] *The Prayse of Nothing* (1585; reprinted 1862), p. 17.

Timon's statement, of course, had its obverse side. Nothing, in a positive sense, did produce all things; and its formidableness in the genesis of man's affairs and dreams became for Shakespeare, as for his contemporaries, a fertile obsession. Shakespeare's meditation on this orthodox theme runs through such forms as Romeo's oxymoronic "O anything, of nothing first create" (I.i.184); Mercutio's rhapsody on the origin of dreams (I.iv.96–103); and even, perhaps, whole plays in which the dramatist's virtuosity was demonstrated by the extent to which he could make something of nothing.

But possibly the aspect of the subject that most fascinated Shakespeare, judging from his references to it, was its metaphorical application to the poet's craft. According to the psychological authority Laurentius, "the understanding part of the minde receiveth from the imaginative the formes of things naked and voide of substance." [17] This, the creative shaping of what was trifling, insubstantial, or unknown, seems to have impressed Shakespeare as the real challenge facing the imagination. In his most famous lines on the subject (*A Midsummer-Night's Dream* V.i.14–17), he speaks of imagination bodying forth the forms of things unknown, while the poet's pen

[17] M. Andreas Laurentius, *A Discourse of the Preservation of the Sight* (1599); Shakespeare Assoc. Fac. no. 15, p. 16. For the relationship between the understanding and the imagination, see Thomas Wright, *The Passions of the Minde* (1601), pp. 91–96.

Turns them to shapes, and gives to airy nothing
A local habitation and a name.

Nor is the task of shaping "airy nothing" peculiar
to the poet. It is shared by all who imagine. Ophelia's
"speech is nothing,"

Yet the unshaped use of it doth move
The hearers to collection.

(Hamlet IV.v.8)

Here it is the hearers who turn the nothing, the nonsense, into shapes. And Shakespeare demanded that
his audience generally do the like. The audience's obli-
gation to give the actors thanks for nothing, as pro-
posed by Theseus, is best explained by the playful
demands of the mock encomia. But in *Henry V* Shakespeare challenges the audience more seriously. Let us
actors, he asks,

> ciphers to this great accompt,
> On your imaginary forces work.[18]

Nothing is the material of human dreams. Mercutio,
like Gonzalo accused of talking of "nothing," also
shapes the word to his own ends:

[18] *Henry V* Prologue, 17. See Alwin Thaler, "Shakespeare
on Style, Imagination, and Poetry," *Publications of the Modern
Language Association,* LIII (1938), 1031.

> True, I talk of dreams,
> Which are the children of an idle brain,
> Begot of nothing but vain fantasy,
> Which is as thin of substance as the air.[19]

Imogen describes her supposed dream as "but a bolt of nothing, shot at nothing, / Which the brain makes of fumes" (*Cymbeline* IV.ii.300–301). Distempered fantasies are similarly begot. Queen Isabella, fainting from "heavy nothing" (or could it be heavy noting?), is told by Bushy, " 'Tis nothing but conceit, my gracious lady." Her reply, though hysterical and equivocal, is in one of its senses consistent with Shakespeare's other statements on the theme:

> 'Tis nothing less: conceit is still deriv'd
> From some forefather grief; mine is not so,
> For nothing hath begot my something grief,
> Or something hath the nothing that I grieve.
> (*Richard II* II.ii.34)

One must not, of course, try to build Shakespeare's concept of imaginative creation upon the fanciful, and at best figurative, references to Nothing in these passages. At the same time, analogy with the doctrine of divine creation, which was neither fanciful nor figura-

[19] *Romeo and Juliet* I.iv.96. "Affection," states Leontes in a wild speech, communicates with dreams and "fellow'st nothing," but may "co-join with something" (*The Winter's Tale* I.ii.138–143).

tive, helps to explain the remarkable persistence with which the concept of nothingness, and usually the word itself, appears in his statements on poetry and dreams. And it is interesting that Puttenham should use, "reverently" he is careful to add, analogy with the Christian God to justify the Greek notion of the poet as maker (rather than simply imitator). Did not God, "without any travell to his divine imagination," make "all the world of nought"? [20]

But perhaps enough has now been said about Nothing to give point to the title of this chapter: Did Shakespeare intend the *Nothing* in *Much Ado About Nothing* to have what was for him a characteristic richness and emphasis?

More than a century ago, Richard Grant White employed his knowledge of Elizabethan English in a bold proposal that the original audience both pronounced and interpreted the title as "Much Ado About Noting"; for noting, or observing and eavesdropping, is found in almost every scene and is indispensable to all the plots.[21] Although no successful refutation of White's

---

[20] George Puttenham, *The Arte of English Poesie* (1589), in *Elizabethan Critical Essays,* ed. G. Gregory Smith (Oxford, 1950), II, 3. This analogy, potentially more serious in poetics than can be shown here, is absent from even so sound a study as M. W. Bundy's " 'Invention' and 'Imagination' in the Renaissance," *Journal of English and Germanic Philology,* XXIX (1930), 535–545.

[21] *The Works of William Shakespeare,* ed. R. G. White (Boston, 1857), III, 226–227.

argument has appeared, its rejection is implicit in an almost perfect editorial silence. Not only do most editors fail even to mention the theory (Hardin Craig is apparently unique in mentioning it, in a footnote), but there has been only the most casual of commentary on the title.[22]

Possibly some of the additional evidence needed by White is now before us. He proved that *noting* yielded a good reading of the play; he could not prove that Shakespeare intended so slight a title to carry weight. With our awareness of the various Nothing discourses, of their challenge to make as much as possible of *nothing,* of Shakespeare's concept of nothing as the material of imaginings, and of his tendency to underline the word, we can add support to White's theory—though only by correcting his exclusive emphasis on the meaning of "noting."

Writers who ingeniously shaped Nothing into many significances did employ the pun, but their medium demanded the use of other kinds of manipulation than punning. In attempting a *dramatic,* rather than expository, elaboration, Shakespeare would give the playwright's equivalent of the poet's imaginative shaping.

[22] For example, the twelve pages devoted to the play in T. M. Parrott's *Shakespearean Comedy* (New York, 1949) bear no allusion to the title. Most editors who do allude to it (Neilson and Hill, O. J. Campbell, and G. B. Harrison) refer to it either as a symptom of genial carelessness or as a clue that all will turn out happily.

Out of a trifle, a misunderstanding, a fantasy, a mistaken overhearing, a "naughtiness," might come the materials for a drama—as happened, less deliberately perhaps, in *King Lear*.

Besides paying deserved respect to an important word, this theory has the merit of removing from the most troublesome of Shakespeare's happy comedies many of the supposed imperfections in character and motivation. At worst, perhaps, it will move the hearers to collection.

CHAPTER III

Hotspur's "bright Honour"

Of the ways in which Shakespeare reshaped and aug-
mented his sources to give unity to *1 Henry IV*, one
of the most deliberate is his elaboration, through word
and character, upon the theme of military honor.[1]
Honor, in fact, becomes a major word in the play. Although Falstaff, Vernon, Prince Hal, Douglas, and
the King participate in developing the theme of honor,
Hotspur by his devotion to "bright Honour" (I.iii.
202) represents the theme itself. He judges his fellows
by their response to "so honourable an action" (II.iii.
36). By other characters he is seen as "the theme of

---

[1] For a broader study of honor in the Elizabethan drama, including the many nuances of the word but not including the
material in this chapter, see C. L. Barber, *The Idea of Honour
in the English Drama 1591–1700* (Göteborg, 1957) and Curtis
Brown Watson, *Shakespeare and the Renaissance Concept of
Honor* (Princeton, 1960).

Honour's tongue" (I.i.81), "the king of honour" (IV. i.10), and the "child of honour and renown" (III.ii. 139). His slaughter of the Scots and capture of prisoners represents "an honourable spoil" (I.i.74), and against Douglas he has gained not simply victory, but "never-dying honour" (III.ii.106).

Shakespeare's exceptional interest in the subject at this time may not seem strange in view of the many contemporary military adventurers whose ambitions were almost limitless. But the repeated use of the word *honor* in this play, often in verse that strikes us as hyperbolic, suggests a verbal, possibly a literary, significance, rather than an immediate representation of the personality of men such as Drake, Hawkins, and Essex.[2] This tendency may be explained, I believe, by reference to a body of literature intermediate to the play and the actual Elizabethan heroes—a body of

---

[2] Drake and Hawkins were businessmen as well as adventurers. Essex, the man most commonly identified with Hotspur, reveals in his speech and writings a complex and civilized temperament. In 1595 he was writing to the Earl of Rutland: "To praise knowledge, or to persuade your L. to the love of it, I shall not need to use many words; I will only say, that, where that wants, man is void of all good; without it there can be no fortitude, for all other darings come of fury, and fury is a passion, and passions ever turn into their contraries; and therefore the most furious men, when their first blaze is spent, be commonly the most fearful" (W. B. Devereux, *Lives and Letters of the Devereux, Earls of Essex* [London, 1853], I, 327). Although Essex was undoubtedly impetuous, it is possible that his popular reputation was in part given him by propagandists and journalists—like those to be considered in this chapter.

literature so considerable in quantity and so distinctive in tone that a popular dramatist could have echoed its manner with assurance of easy recognition.

I refer to the hortatory and gratulatory tracts flourishing between 1589 and 1597 which were devoted to idealizing the English soldiers and seamen who conducted raids on Spanish territory and shipping.[3] The character of these tracts is suggested by Peele's line, "War's laud is matter for the brazen trump."[4] They may seek, as does *A True Coppie of a Discourse*,[5] to arouse dull-minded serving men and courtiers to leave their "soft unprofitable pleasures" and earn "true honour" against the Spaniards, or they may solicit due acclaim for adventurers like Drake and Hawkins; their style is generally too high in pitch for our tastes, and their reference to honor, insistent and shrill. Just as Hotspur and his "bright Honour" were an anachronism in a military scene dominated by Falstaff, con-

---

[3] Except for Louis B. Wright's article on one of the men responsible for them ("Henry Robarts: Patriotic Propagandist and Novelist," *Studies in Philology*, XXIX [1932], 176–199), these tracts have received slight recognition. The present account may serve to counterpoise R. V. Lindabury's disclosure that "seamen engaged in hazardous enterprises got small glory from their exploits in the plays" (*A Study of Patriotism in the Elizabethan Drama* [Princeton, 1931], p. 165).

[4] George Peele, "An Eglogue Gratulatorie," line 33, in *The Works*, ed. A. H. Bullen (London, 1887).

[5] Anthony Wingfield, *A True Coppie of a Discourse written by a Gentleman, employed in the late Voyage of Spaine and Portingale* (London, 1589).

scripts, and gunpowder (not to mention the ideal represented by Prince Hal), so these tracts rather hopelessly attempt to further the cause of restoring a vocabulary of chivalry to an age wherein the realistic language of battle had little relevance to outmoded terms like *honor*.

The verse of George Peele expresses the early excitement of this cause, for most of it appeared soon enough to escape the later ridicule and satire (as in Beaumont and Fletcher). In *A Farewell. Entituled to the famous and fortunate Generalls of our English force: Sir John Norris & Syr Frauncis Drake Knights, and all theyr brave and resolute followers* (1589), he exhorted English manhood: "Change love for arms; girt-to your blades, my boys!" (line 10). The reward is honor:

> All honours do this cause accompany;
> All glory on these endless honours waits:
> These honours and this glory shall He send,
> Whose honour and whose glory you defend.
> (line 73)

In the same year Peele trumpeted once more, this time to welcome Essex back from the Portugal Expedition. In "An Eglogue Gratulatorie," the accent on flamboyant honor is akin to that in Hotspur's famous outburst:

O honour's fire, that not the brackish sea
Mought quench, nor foeman's fearful 'larums lay!
So high those golden flakes done mount and climb
That they exceed the reach of shepherd's rhyme.

(line 148)

Unlike Shakespeare, Peele could write in this style happily unaware of the grotesque quality inherent in such language.

In 1591 appeared *The Honorable Actions of That Most Famous and Valiant Englishman, Edward Glenham* . . . , celebrating this seaman's piratical successes against the Spaniards and the Holy League, and intended as "an encouragement to our English adventurers." But for those who, like Hotspur's correspondent, could not be moved by an honorable action, it held up reproachfully the example of Glenham, who, "scorning the Idle life which many desireth, adventured also his body in this voyage, showing his worthie undaunted minde, which holdeth honour in greater regarde, then ease at home." [6]

Appended to this work are brazen verses by one "H.R.," apparently designed to enforce poetically the moral of the prose tract:

Brave men at Armes, Englands Cheveleers,
Let Glenhams honors, mongst you be of name,

[6] Sig. A 2. Reference is to the reprint by J. Compton (London, 1820).

Whose conquests gainde, gainst Spanish Caviliers,
With goulden Trumpe, eternisd is by fame.

This H.R. was Henry Roberts (or Robarts), a minor
but prolific writer,[7] untiring in the cause of honor. The
representative nature of his work is indicated in *Lan-
caster his Allarums* (1595), which commemorated a
marauding expedition to Brazil and lamented that
"our ungrateful Countreymen . . . holde Honours
Champions in account no longer than the present occasion or use serveth for them" (sig. B 1). In *The
Trumpet o[f] Fame* (1595), he trumpeted a more
confident encouragement to the followers of Drake
and Hawkins:

Such honor now, our hope is [God] will send.
Take courage then, let honor be your aime,
And drag not back, you that will honor gaine.
At your returne, then shall you honor have,
As your deserts by venturing farre shall crave.

(p. 5)

Verse of comparable vigor and variety was produced as late as 1596 by Charles Fitzgeffrey in *Sir*

[7] See Wright, *op. cit.* Some of Roberts' "honor" tracts are
*A most friendly farewell . . . to . . . Sir Frauncis Drake
Knight* (1585) ; *Robertes his Welcomme of Good Will to Capt.
Candishe* (1588; not extant) ; *Fames Trumpet soundinge*
(1589) ; *Newes from the Levane Seas* (1594), Roberts' own
tribute to Glenham's exploits; *Honours Conquest* (1593),
largely a chivalric romance.

Francis Drake, His Honorable Lifes Commendation, and his Tragicall Deathes Lamentation. In keeping with the temper of *honor* literature, Fitzgeffrey requests "the quaint tragedians of our time":

> Cease to eternize in your marble verse
> The fals of fortune-tossed Venerists;
> And straine your tragicke Muses to rehearse
> The high exploites of Jove-borne Martialists.
>   (sigs. B 7ᵛ-B 8)

The work was popular, and it may have helped influence Shakespeare to make a nearly tragic character of love-scorning and honor-seeking Hotspur. Besides eulogizing Drake, Fitzgeffrey considers the relationship of rashness and honor, a theme figuring in the portraiture of the impetuous, "hare-brain'd" Hotspur (V.ii.19). Though lamenting the "hare-braind hardiment" of one member of the expedition, he reaches the generous conclusion:

> For if by rashnesse valour have got honour,
> We blame the rashnes, but rewarde the valour.
>   (sig. E 6)

A more thorough examination of the relationship of rashness to honor is made by Gervase Markham in a similar work, *The Most Honorable Tragedie of Sir Richard Grinvile, Knight* (1595). Grenville, the hero

of the *Revenge,* is exonerated from the charge of fool-
hardiness and saluted as "armes and honors sover-
aigne." Even the Spanish general is moved to tears at
Grenville's death and wishes him lasting renown:

> You powers of heaven, rayne honour on his hearse,
> And tune the Cherubins to sing his fame,
> Let infants in the last age him rehearse,
> And let no more, honour be Honors name.
>
> (sig. G 7)

Fitzgeffrey's and Markham's works, despite the mo-
notony of their shrill eulogizing, are distinguished by
an attempt to express the tragedy as well as the achievement of the heroes' lives.

The foregoing eight works are merely a representative selection of the flood of honor-trumpeting tracts
that excited or disturbed Englishmen in the years when
Henry IV must have been beginning to engage Shakespeare's mind.[8] Meditative spirits may well have given
the matter thought. The theologically minded John
Norden did so in *The Mirror of Honor* (1597),
written to stir military men "to a desire to become also

---

[8] Notable among others is *The Sea-mans Triumph* (1592),
written to accord to men "hauty and full of courage" the "honour
they have deserved, to the encouragement of others" (sig. A 3ᵛ).
George Chapman's genuinely poetic "De Guiana carmen Epicum"
(1596), celebrating "Riches with honour, conquest without
blood," is of a somewhat different type, as are most of the
records of exploration in Hakluyt.

vertuous and obedient to God, and in him to their Prince and Commanders, that as they seeke honor, they may so attaine it, as may make them in deede truely honorable" (sig. B 1ᵛ). Robert Ashley did so in his calm, philosophical treatise *Of Honour* (written in 1596 or shortly thereafter), which represented, in the opinion of its modern editor, "the earliest attempt by an Englishman to deal with the subject comprehensively and systematically in a separate work." [9] Of the attitudes toward honor, Ashley recommends neither that of "the dull and heavye spirited" nor that of men "so eager in the desire thereof that they had more need of a brydle to restraine them from their over hote pursuit, then of spurrs to pricke them forwardes." [10]

The subject of honor was undoubtedly a topic of the day. Equally important for a dramatist, it had received expression in a literary jargon which lent itself well to the patterned, thematic delineation Shakespeare apparently sought in *1 Henry IV*. To Elizabethans of 1597, the man who would pluck "bright Honour" from the moon must have had an accent as familiar and as rich in connotation as that of the earth-bound warrior whom honor could not prick on.

[9] Ed. V. B. Heltzel (San Marino, California, 1947), p. 1.
[10] *Ibid.*, pp. 24, 49.

CHAPTER IV

"Redeeming time" in HENRY IV

In *Henry IV*, particularly Part I, the word that is most commonly assumed to have central importance is *honor*. It was, as we have seen, a word figuring prominently in English life and literature in the period when *Henry IV* was written. Nevertheless, although *honor* (including its derivatives) appears twenty-nine times in *1 Henry IV* and eight times in *2 Henry IV*, the word *time* (excluding derivatives) [1] has forty-one appearances in the first part and thirty-four appearances in the second. It has the added distinction of being talked about in crucial episodes.

Hal in his famous soliloquy promises:

[1] There are also some sixty-four references to units of time in the two plays.

I'll so offend, to make offence a skill,
Redeeming time when men think least I will.
(I.ii.239)

Falstaff, significantly, says little about time, except for
reluctant acknowledgments that he is growing old. He
tries futilely, in what I think is his only real mental
conflict, to ignore time. But it catches up with him
humiliatingly when Hal rejects him as "old man" and
remarks, "How ill white hairs become a fool and
jester!" (*2 Henry IV* V.v.51–52). Hotspur, in sharp
contrast, is driven by a passionate time-consciousness.
He wonders how his father has the leisure to be sick.
He pleads with his fellow rebels: ". . . yet time
serves wherein you may redeem / Your banish'd honours . . ." (*1 Henry IV* I.iii.180–181). As he approaches the moment of his death he achieves some
of the finest perceptions in the play on the subject of
time. There is his anguished, but theologically war-
ranted, exclamation:

O gentlemen, the time of life is short!
To spend that shortness basely were too long,
If life did ride upon a dial's point,
Still ending at the arrival of an hour.
(*1 Henry IV* V.ii.82)

And in his dying speech there occurs what Aldous
Huxley has called one of the most profound observations on life ever made by Shakespeare:

But thoughts, the slaves of life, and life, time's fool,
And time, that takes survey of all the world,
Must have a stop.

(*1 Henry IV* V.iv.81)

So important, in fact, is *time* in *Henry IV* that one might accept as the motto for the two parts of the play the observation made by Hastings: "We are Time's subjects, and Time bids be gone" (*2 Henry IV* I.iii.109).

The emphasis on the concept of time was not, of course, unique with *Henry IV*. Viewed against the background of Shakespeare's other plays written within a few years of *Henry IV*, this emphasis appears to be part of a long-range concern with the meaning and wise use of time. It is noticeable in the antecedent play, *Richard II*, where, as apparently in *Henry IV*, the central character wastes time. Richard laments that because he has wasted time, time wastes him. But the play itself does not justify Richard's own view of his tragedy. The concept of time remains external to the play and does no more than testify to the impression that it was beginning to engage the dramatist's own mind. However, in *As You Like It, Hamlet,* and *Troilus and Cressida,* time is not merely talked about; it becomes a part of the dramatic action. The concept of time becomes increasingly meaningful throughout Shakespeare's plays. I will devote my discussion here to only one play (and I think that what I have to say will prove that it *is* one play), *Henry IV*.

The primary emphasis given to *time* in *Henry IV* is the problem of its redemption. Hal promises in his soliloquy to redeem time when men think least he will. Since this soliloquy is commonly accepted as Shakespeare's vehicle for telling the audience directly about the play, the ringing couplet concluding it is of thematic importance. Unfortunately, as though the soliloquy in its own right were not perplexing enough, critics have enriched the difficulty by failing to give any real thought to what Hal (and Shakespeare) meant by "redeeming time." As a result, the soliloquy and, inevitably, both parts of the play have been misinterpreted.

It is indicative of the casual editorial treatment of the phrase, and also a good example of the way editors avoid precise plagiarism, that every editor has said essentially the same thing in glossing the passage, but has taken the pains only to change a word or so from the gloss used by his predecessors. The English Arden edition has "making amends for time misspent"; G. L. Kittredge, "making up for time wasted"; Dover Wilson, "making up for time misspent"; O. J. Campbell, "making amends for the time I have lost"; and M. A. Shaaber, "atoning for time misspent." No two are identical; all, I am convinced, are essentially wrong.

Editors of the play seem to have failed to notice—

even though one or two refer the reader to Ephesians
5:16 for clarification—that there was a considerable
body of contemporary religious literature illuminating
the expression and underlining its importance for Shakespeare and his audience. There was even a sermon by
one William Whately (whom Shakespeare may well
have known) called *The Redemption of Time* (1606).
Reference to only a few of these religious works would
have preserved editors from the pitfall of believing
that "redeeming time" meant "making up for lost
time." I have found only one Elizabethan writer who
seemed to believe this feat possible. The others indi-
cate not only that it was impossible but that the expression had quite a different meaning.

Let us first examine the evidence showing that time
lost was considered hopeless of redemption. John
Carpenter, in a typical monitory work called *Time
Complaining* (1588), says this of those who have
misspent their time:

> The benefit of their time also they either do not
> knowe, or have forgotten it: for they endevor not
> to use her, but every way to abuse her, and wast
> out the time in their worldlie vanities, which being
> once let gon is never recalled againe.
>
> (sig. A 5)

William Jewel, in *The Golden Cabinet of True Treas-
ure* (1612), says that those of us who waste our min-

utes "shal find them to be a great diminution of our
dayes; whose redemption being hoplesse, they doe
leave in our soules a wofull remembrance that they
once past by" (p. 64). And Roger Matthew, in another
discomfiting work, *The Flight of Time* (1634), offers
the only advice possible to those who have misspent
time (p. 10): to "plucke our selves by the ear for
every lost day, and redeeme the next." This last quota-
tion in particular makes it clear that "redeeming" a
day meant something quite distinct from making
amends for it and that Prince Hal cannot, as the future
"mirror of all Christian kings," be hoping to make
atonement for months of debauchery by a sudden reform.

What, then, was the widely understood meaning of
"redeeming time"? Clearly it had some reference to
the passage from Ephesians. And there were two popular means of disseminating this source. One was through
the religiously directed drama. In *Lusty Juventus,* a
crude precursor of *Henry IV,* Good Counsel tells Lusty
Juventus:

> Saint Paul unto the Ephesians giveth good exhorta-
> tion,
> Saying, walk circumspectly, redeeming the time,
> That is, to spend it well, and not to wickedness in-
> cline.[2]

[2] In Robert Dodsley, *A Select Collection of Old English
Plays* (4th ed.; London, 1874–1876), II, 49–50.

It is worth noting, however, that Lusty Juventus has failed principally—with a significance which will appear later—to expend his time in the pursuit of wisdom. He is not, any more than is Hal, guilty of "wickedness."

Another vehicle of wide popular dissemination of the source was the Homilies. Whether or not Shakespeare's audience ever read a single book of religious exhortation, they could not have escaped the following instruction included in "The Third Part of the Homily for Rogation Week": "St. Paul willeth us *to redeem the time, because the days are evil.* It is not the counsel of St. Paul only, but of all other that ever gave precepts of wisdom." "There is," concludes the Homily, "no precept more seriously given and commanded." ³

The passage from *Lusty Juventus* is typical in pointing to the meaning of the phrase as spending present time well, not that of trying to recover or atone for the time of days past. This meaning is clarified by a passage from a sermon by the popular preacher Henry Smith: "Let us redeeme the day which wee have foreslowed, so many dayes, wherein we have so long hardned our hearts: let us take up this day and make

³ *Certain Sermons Appointed by the Queen's Majesty to be declared and read by all parsons, vicars, and curates, every Sunday and holiday in their churches . . . Newly Imprinted in Parts according as is mentioned in the book of Common Prayers* (1574), ed. G. E. Corrie (Cambridge, England, 1850), p. 492. [Henceforth cited as Corrie.]

it the day of our repentance."[4] Matthew speaks to
similar purpose in *The Flight of Time* (p. 10) : "Labour we by prayer and repentance and new obedience,
to make our evill daies good daies, and so to rescue and
recover our time into its liberty again." It should be
observed that by "evill daies" Matthew does not mean
past days, but rather the inherently sinful days of this
life, which he refers to on the title page as "the sad
time of this mortalitie."

Thus, to the Elizabethan audience, to redeem (or
"rescue") time would be clearly understood as meaning to take full advantage of the time that man is given
here on earth for salvation. The godly, said Adam Hill
in a sermon at Paul's Cross in 1593, "labour earnestly
in their vocations in this precious, short, and irrevocable
time of their life, because after death there is no daye,
but night, no time accepted, but the daye of venge-
ance."[5] The wicked, according to the Homily already
cited, abuse this short period of life, and "therefore do
the godly take the better hold of the time, to redeem it
out of such use as it is spoiled in by the wicked."[6] Shakespeare had earlier stated through the mouth of Valen-

[4] *Ten Sermons Preached by Maister Henry Smith* (1596),
sig. R 3ᵛ.

[5] *The Crie of England* (1595), p. 67. This sermon was published at the request of the Lord Mayor.

[6] Corrie, p. 492. See also Thomas Becon, "A New-Year's
Gift," in *Early Writings* (Cambridge, England: Parker Society
1843), p. 326.

tine in *The Two Gentlemen of Verona* the potential tragedy of a youth who does as Prince Hal seems to do,

> Omitting the sweet benefit of time
> To clothe mine age with angel-like perfection.
>
> (II.iv.65)

It may be objected that although Shakespeare must have known and probably accepted the orthodox concept of time given for redemption, *Henry IV* does not strike us today as a play with much religious meaning. It is true that Falstaff quotes the Bible probably more than does any other Shakespearian character and that he repeatedly raises the question of repentance. But the idleness of Prince Hal does not seem to be a trait that imperils his soul. This is, indeed, the point made most ably by Dover Wilson, the only critic who gives serious attention to the theological meaning of the play.

Wilson rightly turns for possible theological meaning to the speculations about Hal's reform made by the bishops in *Henry V*. Shakespeare has given the bishops a lengthy and, to us, rather tedious prominence. Yet, according to Wilson, the prelates

> say nothing about religion except that he is "a true lover of the holy church" and can "reason in divinity"; the rest of their talk, some seventy lines, is concerned with learning and statecraft. . . . If Hal had sinned, it was not against God, but against Chiv-

alry, against Justice, against his father, against the interests of the crown. . . . Instead of educating himself for the burden of kingship, he had been frittering away his time.

Wilson concludes that "repentance in the theological sense, repentance for sin, is not relevant to his case at all." [7]

It can, however, be demonstrated that if he was "frittering away his time," Hal was courting—whether he seems so to us or not—a serious theological hazard, and that his very soul was in jeopardy. Editors have too genially dismissed the implication of Hal's statement in his soliloquy:

> I know you all, and will awhile uphold
> The unyok'd humour of your idleness.

Shaaber, for instance, glosses *idleness* as "frivolity." An instructive parallel is that of Spenser's Guyon, and one is not surprised to find a similarly amiable interpretation given by critics to this hero's dallying on the Lake of Idleness. According to De Selincourt, for example, after Guyon has manfully resisted the "violent passions of anger and malignity," he is "seduced for a while by idle pleasures. But Spenser clearly regards

[7] *The Fortunes of Falstaff* (Cambridge, England, 1944), pp. 24, 33.

his defection with sympathetic tolerance; and Sir Guyon suffers no great hurt from his short passage with irresponsible Mirth upon the Lake of Idleness." [8]

However much we may today be inclined to treat indulgently the hazard of idleness in the two cases, dismissing it as a rather attractive frivolity, for the Renaissance audience "idleness" had as rigorous a religious connotation as "redeeming time." In Guevara's very popular work *The Golden Booke of Marcus Aurelius* (1586), idleness is referred to as "the greatest signe of a lost man." Further, "the filth of secret chambers, the stinch of the pump in ships, nor the ordures of cities, do not corrupt the aire so much as idle folke doe the people" (sig. K 1). The church and government felt the subject important enough to warrant "An Homily against Idleness." This Homily announced that it is a sign of man's "corruption of nature through sin" that "he taketh idleness to be no evil at all, but rather a commendable thing." Thus, idleness was undoubtedly "grievous sin" to Shakespeare's audience.[9] Wilson is therefore mistaken in assuming that because Hal is not being actually criminal, his "frittering away" of time had no religious import.

I would especially disagree with Wilson in his dis-

---

[8] *The Poetical Works of Edmund Spenser,* ed. J. C. Smith and E. De Selincourt (London, 1950), p. xliv.
[9] Corrie, p. 516.

missal of Hal's new learned qualities as nontheological accomplishments. Those Renaissance theologians who tell how to redeem the time pay particular attention to self-searching, meditation, and learning as essential means to salvation. Hardin Craig has pointed out that the Reformation brought "the idea that learning was necessary for the hereafter as well as for the here and now. Men were suddenly made responsible for the achievement of their salvation, not a salvation resting on virtue and obedience only, but resting also on comprehension." [10] The pious individual, according to Matthew (p. 11), in order that he shall lose no opportunity for redeeming time, will always be devising "how to imploy this smallest mites of time, some about his honest vocation, other some in hearing, reading, meditating, conferring. . . ." Mr. Ezechiel Culverwell, "worthy Man of God," began sometime about 1595 to compile his helpful volume called *Time Well Spent in Sacred Meditations* (1635), which contains models of the type of reading or meditation that the individual should enjoy when alone. William Whately, in *The Redemption of Time* (1606), designated wisdom as the principal aim of those who would redeem their time. Typical of the growing attempt to make this redemption attractive to all people, Whately advertised in the title of his sermon that he was showing men how to redeem time "comfortably." What he did was

[10] *The Enchanted Glass* (Oxford, 1950), p. 143.

to make the redemption seem possible for men who, engaged in the bustling life of the era, had little chance for reading and meditation.

The "comfortable" method of redeeming time brings us back to the applicability of the theological treatises in defining what Hal actually does in *Henry IV*: he is taking full advantage of the time he has on earth for salvation. He seldom seems very uncomfortable in his pensiveness and, as the bishops perplexedly observe, he seems not to have spent much time in private meditation or study. Now, they agree, "he weighs time / Even to the utmost grain." But in his youth, his companies were "unletter'd, rude, and shallow,"

> His hours fill'd up with riots, banquets, sports,
> And never noted in him any study,
> Any retirement, any sequestration
> From open haunts and popularity.
>
> (*Henry V* I.i.55)

Hal's addiction to "open haunts" and his failure to spend time in private meditation remind one of what Whately says of certain worldlings. Isaiah, he notes (p. 13), cries out on those who used their days in banqueting, good cheer, and merrymaking, "So that there was not time to meditate and thinke on those afflictions whereby God did warne them to repentance and amendement, which is most contrary to the duty of redeeming the time, for all this time is even lost and cast away."

I consider it significant that Shakespeare devotes so much attention to the bishops and to their analysis of Hal's change. They were introduced, I think, to represent the very important clerical view of the subject. Hal's method of redeeming time is disturbingly unorthodox and, with the partial exception of Whately, not the kind that the bishops and their brethren were wont to thunder from Elizabethan pulpits. Shakespeare must have delighted in their discomfiture in this respect as much as in their labored proof that Hal had a claim to the throne of France. But the conclusions they reach are, in both cases, obviously meant to be right. Henry did, in Shakespeare's eyes, have a claim to France and he did, in his own way, redeem the time. It was, moreover, a way that was becoming increasingly popular in an age of business and public activity.

Marveling that "never was such a sudden scholar made," the prelates observe that ". . . the art and practic part of life / Must be the mistress to this theoric" (I.i.32, 51–52). In other words, Hal acquired the fruits of meditation by means of a studious public life. This observation agrees with almost all the facts of *Henry IV*. Warwick, in Part II, emphasizes the studious nature of Hal's participation in the ugly world:

The Prince but *studies* his companions
Like a strange tongue, wherein, to gain the language,
'Tis needful that the most immodest word
Be look'd upon and learn'd; which once attain'd,
Your Highness knows, comes to no further use
But to be known and hated.

(IV.iv.68)

Hal was a fast learner. He was so proficient in mingling with tinkers and other commoners that in only a quarter of an hour he learned to drink with any one of them "in his own language" for the rest of his life (*1 Henry IV* II.iv.18–21). Within a short time he achieved the point of view "of all humours that have showed themselves humours since the old days of goodman Adam to the pupil age of this present twelve o'clock at midnight" (*1 Henry IV* II.iv.104– 107). When, as King, he is insulted by a message from the Dauphin about his frivolity in youth, he shows one of his rare moments of genuine anger; he is enraged at the way the Dauphin ". . . comes o'er us with our wilder days, / Not measuring what use we made of them" (*Henry V* I.ii.267). The Dauphin, like other conventional souls, had misjudged his plainly announced intention of so offending as to make offense a skill. Hal had, in actuality, been expending time with a purpose. He was redeeming the time in much the same educational manner as that described by Sir William Cornwallis, the Younger, three years after the play:

I Come now from discoursing with an Husband-man,
an excellent stiffe slave, without observation, respect,
or civilitie. . . . I have sold him an houre of my
time and have ware for it, good sound principles,
in truth, becomming a better fortune. This time hath
not been lost, for his experience, his learning of Tradition, and his naturall witte hath enformed me of
many things. I have picked out of him good Philosophy and Astronomy and other observations of
Time and of the worlde; all which, though he im-
ployes about durt and allotteth to that end, hinders
not me from making a more worthy use of them.[11]

The churchmen, however incapable they may be of
understanding the unconventionality of Hal's personality, are not entirely unaware that he has prospered
spiritually in his own way. They even give him credit
for having ". . . obscur'd his contemplation / Under
the veil of wildness" (*Henry V* I.i.63–64). Through
this explanation they ultimately reject—and so I think
should we—the idea that his reformation came suddenly, that by any single act he made up for lost time.
He grew spiritually, they agree, like the strawberry
underneath the nettle, unseen but "crescive," and growing best by night.

Many critics, I know, believe Hal has redeemed time
when, in Part I, he defeats Hotspur or when, in Part
II, he casts off his followers and becomes a responsible king. These critics make the mistake of which the

[11] Essay. 15. "Of the observation, and use of things," in
Essayes, ed. Don Cameron Allen (Baltimore, 1946), p. 50.

Prince repeatedly accuses those who do not know him well—writing him down after his "seeming." They fail to realize, moreover, that his redeeming of time is going on almost constantly. The two spectacular actions would not have been recognized by the audience as adequate for redemption. For in both of them he has, in the words of his father, "redeemed his lost opinion," not his time; that is, he has merely changed the way people look at him—corrected their false impression given by his "seeming." He has not radically changed his status in the eyes of God. This distinction is well pointed by his statement, "For God doth know, so shall the world perceive" (2 Henry IV V.v.61). God, like the audience, has known from the beginning; it is only the other characters who are surprised by their later perceptions.

But while agreeing with those critics (Shaaber is one of the best of them) who argue that Hal undergoes no radical reform, I do not believe a correct interpretation of "redeeming time" permits us to accept the notion of a static Hal who is perfect from the beginning and is merely enjoying a period of deceiving people, or, even less palatable, that of a Hal who can immerse himself daintily in a world of idle pleasure and emerge the same as he was before. Hal grows as a result of his experiences and not despite them.

What is more, although he is no Hamlet, he undergoes tension and doubt as to the rightness of what he is doing. Occasionally, like Hamlet, he finds himself guilty of purposeless idleness. These are his worst moments. He confesses to Poins, "Well, thus we play the fools with the time, and the spirits of the wise sit in the clouds and mock us" (*2 Henry IV* II.ii.155–157). And again, ". . . I feel me much to blame / So idly to profane the precious time" (*2 Henry IV* II.iv.390–391). That he was poignantly conscious of occasionally wasting time was theologically in his favor. He never grew callous to idleness as Antony was to do.

But on the other hand, he repudiated the terror and limited dogma of the pulpit. To sixteenth-century audiences, both the drama and the humanity in Hal's method of redeeming time must have been far more instructive than the sermons on the subject which, though frightening, they doubtless came to look upon as necessary. Early audiences would have recognized *Henry IV*—both Part I and Part II—as an essay on the subject of redeeming time, but they would also have been at least equally aware that it was a refreshingly different essay. They would have accepted gratefully, with a relaxation of tension which must have been the primary appeal of the play, the realization that time could be redeemed sociably, actively, and interestingly. Their favorite prince had done so.

CHAPTER V

"My name is Pistol call'd"

"It sorts well with your fierceness," [1] comments King
Henry approvingly, upon learning the identity of the
soldier from whom issues the mighty voice. But Henry
seems to have been the last to applaud Shakespeare's
naming of Ancient Pistol. In fact, the New Variorum
edition of *2 Henry IV* (1940) cites in this connection
only attempts to find better reasons than the obvious
for Shakespeare's choice. Two explanations by Halli-
well are offered: (1) Pistail and Bardoulf are names
appearing in a muster roll of artillerymen serving at
the siege of St. Laurens des Mortiers in 1435; (2) the
Italian *pistolfo* is translated by Florio in 1611 as "a
roguing beggar, a cantler, an upright man that liveth
by cosenage." These suggestions show, at least, an

[1] *Henry V* IV.i.63.

awareness that the name must have meant more to Shakespeare than it does to us.

More recently, Leslie Hotson has sought to recapture for modern readers the flavor that once made Pistol rival Falstaff in popularity.[2] Generally successful in this attempt, Hotson nevertheless slights the name of his hero, and thereby misses an interesting source of the ancient's former appeal.

For the pistol does not mean to us what it meant to Elizabethans. It is now the most genteel of firearms; intimate, covert, and sinister in dramatic use—as much at home in the boudoir as in the den. The pistol of the sixteenth century was an unruly, blustering weapon, still in the experimental stage as an abbreviated harquebus, and its use required strength and discretion. "Being overcharged," wrote one veteran officer, "it shakes in a mans hand, so that often it touches neyther man nor horse. If the charge be too little, it pierceth nothing to speake of." [3]

Although firearms in general were slow to gain respect,[4] the pistol, as the most erratic of weapons,

---

[2] "Ancient Pistol," *Yale Review,* XXXVIII (1948), 51–66.

[3] Roger Williams, *A Briefe Discourse of Warre* (London, 1590), p. 36.

[4] "For nearly a century after the invention of fire-arms writers speak disparagingly of them, and, indeed, their effect gave a moral, rather than a physical, superiority to the side using them" (M. J. D. Cockle, *A Bibliography of English Military Books up to 1642 and of Contemporary Foreign Works* [London, 1900], p. 11).

was in a class by itself. "Among those that professe arms," wrote one authority, "it is so assured a principle that a troope of Speares should beate and overthrowe a troope of Pistols, that who so seemeth to doubt thereof is taken to be but a meanly practised souldier."[5] Sir John Smythe, admittedly partial to archery, warned of the pistol's notorious inaccuracy:

> Pistolettiers are not to worke any effect against squadrons or troupes of horsmen or footmen above 10. or 15. yeardes off at the furdest, and if it be enemie to enemie single, then they are not to discharge their peeces above 4. or 5. yardes off; unless they wil faile 5. times, before they hit once, so uncertaine are those weapons of fire.[6]

Smythe refers for support to any captain of experience.

The pistoleer on horseback had a special reputation for inaccuracy. His formidable difficulties are acknowledged by even the most ardent Elizabethan advocate of firearms. The mounted pistoleer, according to Humfrey Barwick, must accustom his horse to "feare neither the cracke nor the fire: and that doone, he must learne to occupie his bridle hande, his Pistoll, and his spurs in due time and forme, all at one instant."[7] Comic pos-

[5] *The Politicke and Militarie Discourses of the Lord de La Noue* (London, 1587), p. 198.

[6] *Instructions, Observations, and Orders Militarie* (London, 1594), pp. 204–205.

[7] *A Breefe Discourse, Concerning the force and effect of all manuall weapons of fire* (London, 1594?), sig. H 3. The fail-

sibilities were evident, and that Shakespeare was not
blind to them is shown in Prince Hal's sarcastic praise
of Douglas as "He that rides at high speed and with
his pistol kills a sparrow flying" (*1 Henry* IV II.iv.
379).

The pistol was not only comically inaccurate; it
often missed fire. In a charge, complained Colonel
Roger Williams, "divers Pistolls faile to goe off." [8]
Sir John Norris had occasion to verify this truth in a
newsworthy manner. At the battle of Suthfield in 1587,
the first charge was given by Norris, "who with his
pistoll in his hand offered to discharge it on a brave
man, but his pistoll would not go off, which he seeing,
stroke it on the head of his enemie and overthrew
him." [9] Knowledge of this failing was not confined to
military experts. In *The Atheist's Tragedy* (1609?)
the hero's life is saved because a pistol, aimed from

> so neare
> A distance that he sha' not shunne the blow,

does not perform.[10]

---

ings of a troop of "reiters," or mounted pistoleers, are described
by Sir Charles Oman: "Cases were known where a man shot
crooked, and hit his neighbour, or blew off the ears of his own
horse." *A History of the Art of War in the Sixteenth Century*
(New York, 1937), p. 86.

[8] *A Briefe Discourse of Warre*, pp. 35–36.

[9] John Stow, *The Annales of England* (London, 1605), p.
1233.

[10] *The Plays and Poems of Cyril Tourneur*, ed. J. C. Collins
(London, 1878), I, 103.

The pistol had only one universally acknowledged distinction: its astonishing report. Though smaller than other firearms, it was scarcely less noteworthy for its flashing fire and percussion. It could terrify both man and horse, without hitting either. Sincere tribute to its fearful sound is paid by François de La Noue: "As for the terror of the speare, it is not of so great efficacie as is the astonishment that the pistoll bringeth at the cracke." [11]

Fitting tribute, one might add, for Ancient Pistol, whose only military usefulness was in his "killing tongue" (*Henry V* III.ii.36). Though his boy marvels at hearing "so full a voice issue from so empty a heart" (*Henry V* IV.iv.71), did not this voice terrify an enemy into submission, and did it not discharge (*Henry V* III.vi.66) "as prave words at the pridge as you shall see in a summer's day"? [12]

[11] *The Politicke and Militarie Discourses,* p. 199.

[12] The obvious physiological associations of *pistol* need no gloss for any audience of typical alertness in such matters, but the reader may wish to consult Eric Partridge's *Shakespeare's Bawdy* (London, 1947), p. 166. Apart from a scene or so in *2 Henry IV,* these associations add little to the characterization of Ancient Pistol which is not conveyed by the military context of his name. I do not, of course, overlook the hilarious obscenity inherent in the sexual connotation, but I do not think of Pistol as primarily an obscene character study.

CHAPTER VI

Noble in CORIOLANUS

Criticism of Shakespeare's Roman plays has overlooked a clue to dramatic meaning which I have learned to view with respect; namely, the preponderant use of a key word. For the Roman plays, the word is *noble*. A few critics, notably Willard Farnham,[1] have made us helpfully aware that the concept of nobility is evident in Shakespeare's later tragedies; but no attempt has been made to discover Renaissance connotations of the word itself. As a result, although Antony's eulogy of Brutus is well known, no one has made clear just why Brutus is the noblest Roman of them all or why this eulogy should serve as a conclusion of the play. Similarly, in *Coriolanus,* critics frequently quote as the explanation of the hero's tragedy that his nature is "too noble for the

---

[1] *Shakespeare's Tragic Frontier: The World of His Final Tragedies* (Berkeley and Los Angeles, 1950).

world," and yet no two critics will agree as to what Shakespeare meant here by *noble*. Indeed, only one (O. J. Campbell, in *Shakespeare's Satire*) has specifically asked what it tells us about Coriolanus' true nature. To achieve some concentration on a single work, I am limiting my survey primarily to *Coriolanus*. But it should be observed that *Julius Caesar* and *Antony and Cleopatra* likewise prove to be dramatic essays on the subject of true nobility; and what I have to say about the connotations of the word may lead to speculations about these plays also.

It is understandable that Shakespeare should seize upon the word *noble* as a thematic word for the Roman plays. Plutarch's *Lives* had been translated by North as *The Lives of the Noble Grecians and Romans* (1579), and in his address to the reader, Amyot remarked that "the immortal praise and glory wherewith [history] rewardeth well-doers is a very lively and sharp spur for men of noble courage and gentlemanlike nature to cause them to adventure upon all manner of noble and great things."

Rome was specially regarded as the place of noble breed. It was, according to Osorio, "the noblest city that ever was." [2] Richard Reynolds called his Roman history *A Chronicle of all the Noble Emperours of the Romans* (1571). Shakespeare was fully aware of the

---

[2] Osorio da Fonseca, *The Five Bookes of Civill and Christian Nobilitie,* tr. William Blandie (1576), sig. B 2.

equivalence of Rome and nobility. *Titus Andronicus* was entered in the Stationers' Register in 1594 as "a noble Roman Historye." Cleopatra sums up the attitude in preparing for a noble Roman death:

> . . . and then, what's brave, what's noble,
> Let's do it after the high Roman fashion.
>
> (IV.xv.86)

It was not, then, accidentally that Shakespeare used the word so often and so pointedly in the three great Roman plays. Nor was it simply because he found it in Plutarch. In *Coriolanus* a comparison between source and play is possible, since only one Life is involved and since Shakespeare and Plutarch cover approximately the same events. In North's Plutarch there are fifty uses of the word in telling the story of Coriolanus, and these are mainly nonconnotative references to the nobility. Shakespeare, in less space, uses the word eighty-five times, and often in a way that raises a question concerning its true meaning.

In questioning the meaning of the word, Shakespeare was following a common practice of the time. Richard Mulcaster impatiently sums up much of the controversy over meaning that took place in the sixteenth century:

> Neither will I rip up what some write of nobilitie in generall, whether by birth or discent: nor what other write of true nobilitie, as disclayming it in that

which vertue avaunceth not: nor what other write of learned nobilitie, as accounting that simply the best, where vertue and learning do beautify the subject. One might talke beyond enough, and write beyound measure, that would examine what such a one saith of nobilitie in greeke, such a one in latin, such in other severall toungues, bycause the argument is so large, the use of nobilitie streaching so farre, and so brave a subject cannot chuse but minister passing brave discourses.[3]

"Passing brave discourses" of this sort were so numerous that I will name but a few. Lawrence Humphrey's *The Nobles or of Nobilitye* appeared in 1563. In 1576 William Blandie translated Osorio da Fonseca's discourse *The Five Bookes of Civill and Christian Nobilitie,* which was advertised as particularly profitable for "the noble Gentlemen of England." At about the time *Coriolanus* was being written, George Meriton preached and published *A Sermon of Nobilitie* (1607), and James Cleland issued *The Institution of a Young Noble man* (1607). Besides these volumes, there were others that contained sections dealing with nobility.[4]

From the point of view of dramatic influence, one of

---

[3] *Positions* (1581), p. 196.
[4] E.g., Giles Corrozet, *Memorable Conceits of Divers Noble and famous personages of Christendome of this our moderne time* (1602), chap. 16, "Of Nobleness and magnanimity"; Annibale Romei, *The Courtiers Academie,* tr. I.K., chap. 5, "Of Nobilitie"; Guillaume de La Perrier, *The Mirrour of Policie* (1596), including a short treatise on nobility.

the most interesting treatises on the subject is a work
in dialogue form by Giovanni Battista Nenna called
*Nennio, or a Treatise of Nobility: Wherein is dis-
coursed what true Nobilite is,* which was translated
into English in 1594 by William Jones. The subject
matter is a traditional one of birth versus desert in
determining true nobility, and, equally conventional,
the case is heavily weighted in favor of desert. Perhaps
the most direct and didactic treatment of the subject in
dramatic form was Henry Medwall's *Fulgens & Lucres*
(*ca.* 1497), a play based upon *De Vera Nobilitate,* a
Latin *controversia* by Bonaccorso, which had been translated into both French and English. Though Medwall's
play is obviously didactic, it may have influenced later,
more artistic works such as Shakespeare's, wherein the
didactic element has been obscured for us by the brilliance of characterization but is nevertheless, if we are
prepared for it, still basic to the meaning of the play.

Because so many of the earlier works on the subject
were in the form of a dialogue, a dispute, or a drama and
were usually concerned with providing the answer to
the question "What is true nobility?" we could predict
that future dramatic works emphasizing nobility would
have a questioning or testing purpose. *Noble* did, in
fact, almost always carry a connotation testing the
validity of its application. If it is applied to a character,
it is usually a signal to the reader or audience to be
prepared to question whether it is rightly applied. A

clear instance of this pattern occurs in *Measure for Measure* when Angelo, hastily appointed Lord Deputy by the Duke, makes the request that must have seemed natural and important to the entire audience:

> Now, good my lord,
> Let there be some more test made of my metal
> Before so noble and so great a figure
> Be stamp'd upon it.

(I.i.48)

Here, as frequently elsewhere, advantage is taken of the pun upon *noble* as a coin—a usage that would emphasize the question of genuineness.

Evidence that *noble* was habitually applied in a questioning or testing sense is found in Humphrey's *The Nobles or of Nobilitye* (sig. D 4) where it is stated that "al which be and wil be accounted nobles knowe not the reason of theyr names"; for, Humphrey explains, "it is well knowen, this word (Noble) is indifferent, and doubtefull: taken in eyther parte good or yll, deryved of the Grammaryans from the Verb Nosco, whych signifieth to know. Wherby properly it rests in him who is famous eyther for vertue or vice." Another example of the testing connotation of *noble* may be found in Osorio, for he cites as the primary business of his treatise (sig. A 2ᵛ) "to search out diligently . . . what oddes there is betwixt the counterfayt, and lively image of perfect Noblenes."

Finally, it should be remembered that the connotation of noble as a testing term had special applicability
to those who were well born and prided themselves upon
nobility of blood. Miss Ruth Kelso has pointed out that
most of the apologists for the gentleman were interested
less in reassuring him than in making him act in a manner worthy of his birth; that is, vindicating his nobility
by deeds.[5] Spenser's sonnet prefacing Jones's *Nennio*
emphasizes that it is a book for

Whoso wil seeke by right deserts t'attaine
Unto the type of true Nobility,
And not painted shews & titles vaine,
Derived farre from famous Ancestrie.

It is not surprising, therefore, to find heroes like
Brutus and Coriolanus not merely proud of their ancestry but also because of that ancestry particularly
anxious to vindicate their claim to it. Anxiety to prove
themselves truly noble is one of the dominant traits of
Shakespeare's Roman heroes, and it leads the audience
to speculate with them concerning the quality of their
nobility. Even Antony, who for much of the play
struggles only fitfully with his ignoble bondage to Egypt,
rouses himself when he sees Eros prove himself nobler
than he:

[5] *Doctrine of the English Gentleman in the Sixteenth Century,* University of Illinois Studies in Language and Literature,
XIV, (1920), p. 38.

> Thrice-nobler than myself!
> Thous teachest me, O valiant Eros, what
> I should, and thou couldst not. My queen and Eros
> Have by their brave instruction got upon me
> A nobleness in record.
>
> (IV.xiv.95)

In *Coriolanus* the testing of Coriolanus' real nobility
is central. Despite his apparent solidity and strength,
he is an anxious man, overeager to prove himself. He
sins, as he recognizes (I.i.234), in envying Aufidius'
nobility. Even his mother, who has fostered in him the
anxiety to prove worthy, warns him about his anxiety
when it threatens to prove their undoing:

> You might have been enough the man you are,
> With striving less to be so.
>
> (III.ii.19)

The critical problem that his anxiety presents is well
stated by the tribunes when (partly to allay his anxiety
to prove his nobility) he is seeking the consulship:

> If you will pass
> To where you are bound, you must inquire your way,
> Which you are out of, with a gentler spirit,
> Or never be so noble as a consul.
>
> (III.i.53)

There is probably a pun upon *gentler* (which was closely related to the idea of noble), underlining the implication that nobility must show itself as gentlemanlike, and not fierce or boorish, in manners.

The essential test of nobility that Coriolanus must face is whether or not he is serving the public good. The test is put squarely to him by the citizens, who may be blockish but who are here given an insight into what is required. The Fourth Citizen states the paradox that underlies Coriolanus' predicament: "You have deserved nobly of your country, and you have not deserved nobly" (II.iii.94). When Coriolanus sarcastically seeks clarification of his "enigma," the citizen explains: "You have been a scourge to her enemies, you have been a rod to her friends; you have not indeed loved the common people."

Contributing to the public good is, according to all evidence outside the play, a supreme criterion of nobility. It is the quality of Brutus which is singled out for praise by Mark Antony in calling Brutus "the noblest Roman of them all"; for

> All the conspirators, save only he,
> Did what they did in envy of great Caesar;
> He only, in a general honest thought
> And common good to all, made one of them.
>   (V.v.69)

It is the quality emphasized again by Shakespeare in *Henry VIII*, when Surrey earnestly declares:

My Lord of Norfolk, as you are truly noble,
As you respect the common good. . . .
(III.ii.289)

It is the quality that is stressed by all contemporary treatises on nobility. Meriton equates "a noble spirit" with a nature that is "directed not so much to private as to publicke good" (sig. E 1ᵛ). Humphrey states that noblemen, in order to be called "the noblest members and stayes of state," must "serve not so muche theyr pryvate as publick honour" (sig. D 5). And Henry Peacham defines nobility as that distinction conferred upon men who, through "some glorious Action performed," have "been usefull and beneficiall to the Common-wealthes and places where they live." [6]

It is toward this public ideal that Coriolanus has been strenuously directed by his mother since he was a child. Volumnia makes this background crucially clear to the audience. When, she states, her son was but a tender, comely youth,

I, considering how honour would become such a person, that it was no better than picture-like to hang by th' wall, if renown made it not stir, was pleas'd

[6] *The Compleat Gentleman* (1634) ; reprinted with an Introduction by G. S. Gordon (Oxford, 1906), p. 2.

to let him seek danger. . . . Hear me profess sincerely: had I a dozen sons, each in my love alike and
none less dear than thine and my good Marcius, I
had rather had eleven die nobly for their country than
one voluptuously surfeit out of action.

(I.iii.9–27)

It is this desire for public service, and not merely a
class loyalty to the nobility, that motivates the better
part of Coriolanus. Even here, however, one suspects
that he is acting from a motive deeply implanted by
his training, which he can mouth but not fully understand. When he refuses to accept honors for his Corioli
heroism, he betrays his carefully nurtured ideal:

> I have done
> As you have done, that's what I can; induc'd
> As you have been, that's for my country.

(I.ix.15)

The words are right, but later events prove that they
do not come untutored from the heart.

Only when it devolves upon him to earn his nobility
in a nonmilitary manner does he show uneasiness. He
would rather, he complains to his mother, serve his
country in his own way. And this inability to transfer his
service from war to peace, an inability revealing that he
is a soldier more than a citizen, proves his undoing.
First, says Aufidius in analyzing Coriolanus' tragedy, he
was

A noble servant to them, but he could not
Carry his honours even.

(IV.vii.35)

Sicinius, although his judgment of Coriolanus is not
without prejudice, correctly describes public sentiment
toward the banished general:

I would he had continued to his country
As he began, and not unknit himself
The noble knot he made.

(IV.ii.30)

Finally his mother has to warn him, when he has prepared to conquer his native country, that by so doing
he will destroy whatever record of nobleness he has
established for himself. The benefit of persevering
against Rome, she predicts, will be a name "dogg'd
with curses,"

Whose chronicle thus writ: "The man was noble,
But with his last attempt he wip'd it out,
Destroy'd his country, and his name remains
To th' ensuing age abhorr'd."

(V.iii.145)

It is significant that now when, more than ever before,
she wishes to control him, she should direct her strategy
toward the passion for nobility that she has nurtured

in him. This is the only motivation that he can understand.

That Coriolanus has a great appetite for the dignity of nobleness must be reconciled, though this has caused critics much difficulty, with his apparent indifference to honors. Here again, however, the treatises on nobility make the situation understandable. They explain why a man who is studious of nobility, and wishes to obtain it by public service, may nevertheless despise public acclaim. When Coriolanus "kicks at" the spoils of war and "rewards / His deeds with doing them," Menenius comments simply, "He's right noble" (II.ii.134). Coriolanus himself must have known that one of the surest signs of true nobility was indifference to its outer show. Peacham comments to this effect: "Nobility, being inherent and naturall, can have (as the Diamond) the lustre but onely from it selfe" (p. 3). Similarly Du Vair: "To bee short, let us hold this for a maxime, that the fruit of noble actions is sayd to have performed them most nobly, and that vertue cannot finde out of her selfe any recompence sufficient to guerdon her selfe withall." [7]

Coriolanus' carefully studied indifference to the outer show of nobility is reënforced by his conviction that the

[7] *The Moral Philosophy of the Stoicks* (1598), p. 82. Cf. Ben Jonson's *Sejanus:* "It is a note / Of upstart greatness, to observe and watch / For these poor trifles, which the noble mind / Neglects and scorns" (V.viii).

opinion of the populace is worth nothing. For one who
is so essentially proud of nobility, it is outrageous that
the plebs, who give "voices" to create honors, are fickle
and foolish in deciding who is noble. He denounces the
plebs' fickleness even before they have had a chance to
show it in the play:

> With every minute you do change a mind,
> And call him noble that was now your hate.
>
> (I.i.186)

One of the commonplaces of the treatises on nobility
was that the populace had no ability to discriminate
nobility. In a collection of maxims listed under the head-
ing "Of Nobilitie," John Bodenham quotes the following verses:

> As none but Eagles gaze against the Sunne,
> So none but vertuous eyes discern nobilitie.[8]

This opinion is certainly vindicated in *Coriolanus* (as
in *Julius Caesar*). The people call Coriolanus noble one
minute and call the tribunes noble the next (e.g., III.iii.
143). Popular blindness to true nobility is dramatically

---

[8] *Bel-vedere or The Garden of the Muses* (1600), p. 68. Cf.
Nennio: "hereunto the foolish opinion of the vulgar sort doth
easilie cause thee to fall: forsomuch as without any difference at
all, they call those noble men, who have but onely a shadow of
Nobilite, as well as they, who are true noble men" (sig. P 1).
See also Du Vair, pp. 74–75.

illustrated in one of the best scenes in *Coriolanus* when
the banished Roman general presents himself in disguise
at the hearth of Aufidius. The Volscian leader fails to
recognize Coriolanus, but he remarks that the Roman,
even in rags, shows "a noble vessel" (IV.v.67). The
Volscian plebs, on the other hand, think he is merely a
burly beggar. Only later, after their leader has wel-
comed the Roman, do they begin to speculate about the
disturbing visitor, trying now to put into words their
awareness that he was something unusual:

> Nay, I knew by his face that there was something in
> him. He had, sir, a kind of face methought,—I can-
> not tell how to term it.
>
> (IV.v.162)

Nor can any of the other Volscian servingmen "term"
it. The people are not, then, meant to be trustworthy
judges of Coriolanus' nobility. As an officer of the
Capitol remarks, "for Coriolanus neither to care
whether they love or hate him manifests the true knowledge he has in their dispositions, and out of his noble
carelessness lets them plainly see 't" (II.ii.13).

"Noble carelessness," however, introduces a new
connotation of the word *noble;* and I believe it is meant
to be crucially important to Coriolanus' tragedy. In a
positive, heroic sense, it connoted standing up boldly,
even recklessly, for one's ideals. When Coriolanus is

threatened with death by the Roman citizens, he is magnificent in defying them and in choosing "Death on the wheel or at wild horses' heels" (III.ii.2) The reaction of his patrician friends is one of admiration mixed with misgivings, as is hinted at by the rather unenthusiastic response by one nobleman, "You do the nobler." His mother's opinion is more explicitly divided between admiration and censure:

> You are too absolute;
> Though therein you can never be too noble,
> But when extremities speak.
>
> (III.ii.39)

Clearly the word *noble* is associated with a carelessly bold ideal of conduct. With this in mind we can more accurately interpret the famous lines by Menenius in which he explains his friend's tragic flaw:

> His nature is too noble for the world;
> He would not flatter Neptune for his trident,
> Or Jove for 's power to thunder. His heart's his
> 　　mouth;
> What his breast forges, that his tongue must vent;
> And, being angry, does forget that ever
> He heard the name of death.
>
> (III.i.255)

Did or did not Shakespeare admire this aspect of nobleness? Elsewhere he is not entirely unambiguous about it. In *Richard II* the Duchess of Gloucester tries to instill this quality of nobility into the politic and weary Gaunt:

> That which in mean men we entitle patience
> Is pale cold cowardice in noble breasts.
>
> (I.ii.33)

Though the expression is conventional, the context gives it a hint of bravura; moreover, the play as a whole is ambiguous about the righteousness of any bold action. A closer approximation to the situation in *Coriolanus*, and one in which haughty pride is sympathetically depicted, occurs in *2 Henry VI*. Suffolk, urged by a gentleman to plead for his life by speaking fair (much as Coriolanus is asked to do), refuses on the ground that it would be contrary to "true nobility":

> No, rather let my head
> Stoop to the block than these knees bow to any
> Save to the God of heaven and to my king,
> And sooner dance upon a bloody pole
> Then stand uncover'd to the vulgar groom.
> True nobility is exempt from fear.
>
> (IV.i.124)

It is also possible to find other contemporary favorable depictions of men who are "too noble for the world." In *Caesar and Pompey* (1607) Pompey laments his having to sue for mercy. It grieves "a noble hauty mind" to "serve and sue." "Nought," he declares, "to a noble mind more greefe can bring." [9] Similarly, in *A Mirror for Magistrates* there is in the words of Anthony Lord Rivers an insistence that

> A noble hart they say is Lyon lyke,
> It can not couche, dissemble, crouch nor fayn.[10]

This is fairly close to the lament that Coriolanus makes:

> Must I
> With my base tongue give to my noble heart
> A lie that it must bear?

> (III.ii.99)

However, most of the treatises describing true nobility do not advise this reckless, haughty point of view. Ascham lists "stoute wilfulness" as one of the "two greatest enemies to Nobilite." [11] Sir Thomas Elyot exclaims, "Lord god, how they be sore blinded which do wene that haulte countenance is a comelyness of nobilite." [12] Most of the didactic writers for the nobility

---

[9] *The Tragedie of Caesar and Pompey or Caesars Revenge* (Malone Society Reprints, no. 22 [London, 1911]), sig. C 3ᵛ.

[10] Ed. Lily B. Campbell (Cambridge, England, 1938), p. 261.

[11] *The Scholemaster* (1570), in *English Works of Roger Ascham,* ed. William Aldis Wright (Cambridge, England, 1904), p. 206.

[12] *The Governour* (1531), Everyman Library ed. (London, 1937), pp. 130–131.

urge that noblemen be adaptable, even "common," in relations with the citizens. Humphrey urges (sig. N 6ᵛ) : "Towards the multitude eke, and common sort, some duties muste bee observed: that Nobilite maye (as it were) flow, into all mens hertes. To winne them with curtesy, not affray them with cruelty." And Cleland, in a statement that helps to clarify the "too noble for the world" passage, advises noblemen: "It is great wisdom for a man to accommodate himself and to frame his manners apt and meete for al honest conference, and society of men. . . . It is a most rare quality in a Noble man to be common, that maketh him imitate Gods goodness . . ." (pp. 168–169).

Shakespeare theoretically accepted moral doctrine of this sort, and although as a dramatic artist he allowed the dynamic individual to develop beyond the precepts of moral treatises, it is probable that, with a modicum of ambiguity, he intended to say that Coriolanus failed of true nobility partially because he had this nobility to an excess that vitiated it. Largely because of his mother's influence, he had tried too hard.

There is, moreover, still another connotation of "noble carelessness," and it is one almost equally derogatory of a protagonist who would be truly noble. Coriolanus is a person rather easily deceived, almost as easily as "the noble Moor," and the question arises whether for Shakespeare a certain kind of nobility did not carry with it a connotation of credulity and the open heart, of

someone who was so far above using craft that he was
vulnerable to it himself. Such a person is Edgar in *King
Lear* as described by Edmund:

> A credulous father and a brother noble,
> Whose nature is so far from doing harms
> That he suspects none; on whose foolish honesty
> My practices rise easy.
>
> (I.ii.195)

This accords with the definition of nobility given by
Lyly: "the noble minde suspecteth no guile wythout
cause, neither condemneth any wight without proofe"; [13]
and with Jonson's statement in his Dedication of *Vol-
pone:* "but let wise and noble persons take heed how
they be too credulous." One who approximates so guileless a person is Othello, whom Iago delights in calling
noble:

> I would not have your free and noble nature,
> Out of self-bounty, be abused.
>
> (III.iii.199)

The similar gullibility of the noble Brutus is coldly
analyzed by Cassius:

> Well, Brutus, thou art noble; yet, I see,
> Thy honourable metal may be wrought

---

[13] *The Complete Works of John Lyly,* ed. R. Warwick Bond
(Oxford, 1902), I, 218.

From that it is dispos'd; therefore it is meet
That noble minds keep ever with their likes;
For who so firm that cannot be seduc'd?

(I.ii.312)

The credulity implied by the "free and noble nature"
was, for Shakespeare and others, a particularly hazardous attribute of nobility. It might not, to be sure, be un-
favorably applied to a person. In fact, Cavendish had
Cardinal Wolsey use it with emotional force to describe
the uprightness of Norfolk, whom he praises for his
"noble heart":

> Forsooth, Sir, ye do right well deserve to bear in
> your arms the noble and gentle lion, whose natural
> inclination is, that when he hath vanquished any beast,
> and seeth him yielded, lying prostrate before him at
> his feet, then will he show most clemency unto his
> vanquished, and do no harm, nor suffer any other de-
> vouring beast to damage him.[14]

But it must never be forgotten that if successful dealing
with "the world" is expected of true nobility, one cannot be always and splendidly a lion. Nor can noble creatures, in Cassius' phrase, "keep ever with their likes."
Coriolanus must, in the world, deal with the tribunes and
not merely with men of his own sort.

Nevertheless it is not simply a heroic large-minded-

[14] George Cavendish, *The Life of Cardinal Wolsey* (London:
The New Universal Library, n.d.), pp. 140–141.

ness that makes "noble" natures like Othello, Brutus,
Antony, and Coriolanus fail in their ideals. Nor is it
merely credulousness. It is also an imperfect use of
reason; and reason is, as we shall finally see, the *sine
qua non* of true nobility. Nenna writes:

> God framed man into his likeness, to whom he
> graunted not onely being, life, and sence; but he
> added reason therunto, which is a peculiar gift unto
> man. Man being then partaker of all these qualities,
> in which of them shall we place true Nobilitie? cer-
> tainly not in being, nor in life (for that should be
> common with the earth and with the plantes.) Much
> lesse in sence (for then should we make brute beastes
> noble.)
>
> (sig. V 3)

Therefore, he concludes, the "true and perfect nobilitie
of man, consisteth only in that part, which maketh man
different from beastes; and that is reason." [15]

Shakespeare seems elsewhere to have agreed with
this attitude, notably in *Hamlet*. It is explicit in "What
a piece of work is man! How noble in reason!" and likewise in Ophelia's "O, what a noble mind is here
o'erthrown!" wherein she refers to the dissolution of

---

[15] See also Elyot in *The Governour,* who says that of the parts
of the soul the intellectual or understanding part is "of all other
most noble, as whereby man is most like unto God, and is pre-
ferred before all other creatures" (p. 276).

that "noble and most sovereign reason" in the Prince. Perhaps, therefore, the most mistaken statement of nobility is that made by the infatuated Antony when he says of his and Cleopatra's bestial self-indulgence:

> the nobleness of life
> Is to do thus, when such a mutual pair
> And such a twain can do't. . . .
>
> (I.i.36)

But Coriolanus, too, is tragically guilty of failing to use the highest reason. Had he been more reasonable, he would have been able to serve his country well both in war and in peace. That he cannot remain "a noble servant" to his countrymen, that he instead transfers his love to an enemy state, disqualifies him from the highest kind of nobility, just as Brutus is disqualified by yielding to the flattery of his friends and turning his country into a shambles.

Yet Coriolanus, like Brutus, is finally granted the distinction of nobility in death. Because he saves his country from destruction, his name will go down in history as noble. His "honors," as Farnham notes, outweigh his "taints." And the play finally and explicitly answers the question posed by all works dealing with nobility by closing, as does *Julius Caesar,* with emphasis on a noble death. A Volscian lord, representing an objective point of view, pronounces the verdict:

> Let him be regarded
> As the most noble corse that ever herald
> Did follow to his urn.
>
> (V.vi.144)

But one is not allowed to forget that his nobility was imperfect. The words of Aufidius which close the play vindicate Coriolanus' claim to nobility and at the same time hint at his defects as a citizen in both Rome and Antium:

> Though in this city he
> Hath widow'd and unchilded many a one,
> Which to this hour bewail the injury,
> Yet he shall have a noble memory.

The play is, then, an unusually subtle essay on the meaning of true nobility. Shakespeare's answer to the great question is characteristically muted and confused. Coriolanus had served Rome well, and at the same time he had been a vexation to both Rome and Antium. He had seemed to despise public acclaim, and yet had been furious when he was denied official honor. He had been noble in the sense of being guileless and careless, and yet he had carried this to a degree that vitiated his noble standing in the world he lived in. Finally, he had proved unreasonable in almost all matters, trusting to his passions and changing countries when his anger dictated. All in all, he presented a baffling study in a familiar subject. It must have been the inability to answer a positive "yes" or "no" to the question of Coriolanus' true nobility that vexed and excited the audiences of Shakespeare's day.

CHAPTER VII

Hamlet's World of Words

To Polonius' question "What do you read, my lord?"
(II.ii.193) Hamlet replies with what I take to be one
of his most intense utterances: "Words, words, words."
Words surround and engage Hamlet, to such an extent
that *word* becomes a carrier of thematic meaning in the
play. It is not merely that *word* is frequently and em-
phatically used, though usually such a tendency in a
Shakespeare play indicates a more or less conscious
thematic intent. More important, words (as well as all
related references to speech) form a large and oppressive part of the world in which Hamlet moves and seeks
corrective action.

We have largely come to accept Caroline Spurgeon's
analysis of the disease imagery in *Hamlet*. Imagery is
indeed a clue to the author's concept of the play. But the

controlling word, especially in *spoken* drama, seems as good a clue to Shakespeare's intuitive concept of a work. And what is frequently *talked* about in *Hamlet* is not so much disease as speech. One thinks offhand of Polonius' precept to give one's thoughts no tongue (in sharp contrast with his garrulity). Osric's "golden words," Claudius' "most painted word," Laertes' "phrase of sorrow," Gertrude's comforting and pretty words, the skull of the courtier or lawyer that had a tongue in it once, and Hamlet's "words like daggers" as well as his several expressed attitudes toward speech. One remembers finally, as perhaps the most meaningful line in the play, "The rest is silence."

Hamlet lived in a "drossy age," characterized by endless clever euphemistic talk. His attitude toward this falseness closely parallels his surgical approach to the rottenness of society. He advises the players to suit the action to the word, and generally this underlies his objection to the artifices of a society in which ugliness goes disguised in fair-sounding terms—in which he is unctuously called "son" by Claudius, in which his madness is hedged about ceremoniously by Polonius and called "transformation" by Claudius, in which his father's death can be comfortably explained by Claudius and Gertrude, in which Ophelia's suicide can be prettily described as accidental drowning by the Queen, and in which Gertrude's "deed" scarcely shows through the "rhapsody of words" into which she has transformed sweet religion.[1] Hamlet has, therefore, not only a moral murkiness to fight his way through; he has to deal with a linguistic haze that clothes prettily, comfortably, or cleverly all the corruption that he must expose.

His personal taste in speech varies, as we shall see, but mostly he values lack of affectation. He recalls pleasurably the play that others had scorned because "there were no sallets in the lines to make the matter savoury, nor no matter in the phrase that might indict the author of affectation" (II.ii.462). He expresses amused consternation at the verbal fastidiousness of the gravedigger: "How absolute the knave is! We must speak by the card, or equivocation will undo us." [2] Modern women disgust him because, as he tells Ophelia, "You jig, you amble, and you lisp and nick-name God's creatures and make your wantonness your ignorance" (III.i.150). This, he adds with probably more sincerity than has usually been accorded the speech, has made him mad.

The very use of speech, indeed, often seems distasteful to him. Amid all the pleasant, reassuring oratory of

[1] The theme of "seeming" is interestingly described by Maynard Mack, "The World of Hamlet," in *Tragic Themes in Western Literature* (New Haven, Conn., 1960), pp. 39–42.

[2] V.i.148. This sentiment must have been one that Shakespeare himself shared concerning the drossy age. In *The Merchant of Venice* (III.v.48), Lorenzo expresses similar scorn: "How every fool can play upon the word! I think the best grace of wit will shortly turn into silence, and discourse grow commendable in none only but parrots."

the second scene, he is taciturn, answering requests as little as possible and cheapening the King's richest words by punning them into starker form. He is at great pains to swear his friends to silence about the Ghost and his own antic disposition. When he appears disheveled before Ophelia, he speaks not a word, conveying all the range of his misery by gestures and dress. He refuses to be sounded out by Rosencrantz and Guildenstern, though he does compare himself to a recorder which can make excellent music if properly handled.[3] Toward Polonius his attitude is so contemptuous in large part because of the old man's fondness for words. Just as the happiest end for himself seems to be silence, so he judges the end of the garrulous Polonius to be aptly expressed by the old man's surprising silence:

> Indeed this counsellor
> Is now most still, most secret, and most grave,
> Who was in life a foolish prating knave.
> (III.iv.213)

And though Hamlet did not know it, Shakespeare knew with some satisfaction that Polonius had pronounced his own epitaph as he stepped behind the arras: "I'll silence me e'en here" (III.iv.4).

But Hamlet, as we well know, is not simply a taciturn

---

[3] For a good generalization on this episode see Manfred Weidhorn, "Hamlet and the Arts," *Notes & Queries*, n.s., V (1958), 52–53.

hero in a wordy society. He himself contributes gen-
erously toward giving the play more words than any
other Shakespearian work. Silence may be, in an over-
sophisticated society, his ultimate dream of peace. But
he has not always been taciturn, nor during the play is
he always spare of speech or grateful for the circum-
stances that force silence upon him.

Before his father's death and his mother's overhasty
marriage, his had—although we usually prefer not to
acknowledge the fact—been the courtier's tongue. He
must surely have used "golden" words in his courtship
of Ophelia. When Polonius reads aloud Hamlet's ro-
mantic letter and verses, we prefer to think of them as
coming from the "antic" Hamlet: "To the celestial and
my soul's idol, the most beautified Ophelia" (II.ii.109).
It is an "ill phrase," but we cannot easily disregard other
evidence that it came sincerely from Hamlet. There is
no point in ignoring Ophelia's description of his verbal
ardor:

> My lord, he hath importun'd me with love
> In honourable fashion.
>
> . . . .
>
> And hath given countenance to his speech, my lord,
> With almost all the holy vows of heaven
> (I.iii.110–114)

She reproves him for not remembering his "words of
so sweet breath compos'd" (III.i.98); and she recalls,
as she compares his present madness to "sweet bells

jangled, out of tune and harsh," how she had "suck'd the honey of his music vows" (III.i.164).

After seeing the Ghost, moreover, he is anything but silent. He is probably translating a hysterical need for speech into what Horatio calls "wild and whirling words" (I.v.133). Indeed, his newly imposed necessity for secrecy threatens his sanity. Renaissance psychology, like our own, recognized the danger of keeping grief to oneself. In *Macbeth* Malcolm warns the grief-stricken Macduff:

> Merciful heaven!
> What, man! ne'er pull your hat upon your brows;
> Give sorrow words. The grief that does not speak
> Whispers the o'er-fraught heart and bids it break.
> (IV.iii.207)

"Why should calamity be full of words?" asks the Duchess in *Richard III* (IV.iv.126). "Words," answers Queen Elizabeth, "are poor breathing orators of miseries." "Let them have scope!" she advises, for

> though what they will impart
> Help nothing else, yet do they ease the heart.
> (IV.iv.130)

In similar vein Hamlet complains to himself in one of his most poignant lines: "But break my heart, for I must hold my tongue" (I.ii.159).

Hamlet holds his tongue in public so far as direct verbal expression of his grief is concerned. But it is significant that he develops an uncharacteristic taste for passionate speech in drama. Though it offends him to the soul "to see a robustious periwig-pated fellow tear a passion to tatters," he now demands that the player give him "a passionate speech" (II.ii.451), and obviously he uses the emotional experience as an outlet for his own feelings. Evidence of his pent-up emotion (which he mistakenly assumes to be inadequate to the occasion) is offered by his comments upon the player's speech:

> What would he do,
> Had he the motive and the cue for passion
> That I have? He would drown the stage with tears
> And cleave the general ear with horrid speech. . . .
> (II.ii.586)

Hamlet does permit himself this "horrid speech" in his soliloquies. But, even though they are private utterances, they disgust him in their womanly effusiveness. It is "most brave," he reflects after the stormiest of them, that he should unpack his heart with words.

Generally he is indeed "most brave"—in a very true sense—in the hardest part of his mission: maintaining silence concerning his emotion. Though the Renaissance audience might view him, as he views himself, as a slave to the passion of grief, it would also have considered him extraordinarily courageous in controlling public expression of it in words. It is largely because he has painfully disciplined himself in this regard that he

resents so deeply Laertes' verbal display at the grave
of Ophelia:

> What is he whose grief
> Bears such an emphasis, whose phrase of sorrow
> Conjures the wand'ring stars and makes them stand
> Like wonder-wounded hearers?
>
> (V.i.277)

He too, if he let himself go, could "mouth" and "rant"
equally furiously.

Though Hamlet does not give public verbal expression to his grief, he does do what Renaissance moral
philosophers recommended as the lesser of two evils:
he converts his grief to anger. "Let grief / Convert to
anger," Malcolm advises Macduff (*Macbeth* IV.iii.
228). Macduff does so, in both word and deed. He
"blunts not the heart" but "enrages it." Similarly, Hamlet eases his melancholy with angry words—"words like
daggers" as his mother calls them when he has turned on
her (III.iv.95). He chooses angry words against his
mother mainly because he cannot resort to angry deeds:

> I will speak daggers to her, but use none.
> My tongue and soul in this be hypocrites;
> How in my words soever she be shent
> To give them seals never, my soul, consent!
>
> (III.ii.414)

This frustrates him particularly because of his desire
to suit the action to the word. But Gertrude is, fortu-

nately, capable of being shocked by brutal words. She hears for the first time ugliness called by its proper name, her husband referred to not as "my excellent liege" or as the mainstay of the state but as "A murderer and a villain! / A slave . . ." (III.iv.96). Hamlet possesses, to a degree that shocks the word-complacent state, the ability praised by Plutarch in his discussion on "Intemperate Speech or Garrulity." Commending mainly the great virtue of silence, Plutarch does admit the worthiness of those "skilful and well-practised archers and darters, who have the feat of shooting arrows and lancing darts; for they know how and when to speak graciously and bitterly, soundly, pithily, and compactly." [4]

His ability in "lancing darts" is, aside from a reproachful silence, Hamlet's main linguistic contribution to his corrupt society. He calls the king a thing—of nothing. The Queen's relationship with Claudius is not holy marriage, but living

> In the rank sweat of an enseamed bed,
> Stew'd in corruption, honeying and making love
> Over the nasty sty. . . .
>
> (III.iv.92)

The ceremonious and venerable Polonius is a "great baby . . . not yet out of his swathing-clouts" (II.ii.

[4] *Moralia,* tr. Philemon Holland (London, 1936), p. 265.

399). And the fashionable Osric is no more than a water fly. For those who, like Rosencrantz, cannot feel the poniardlike thrust of his cruel words, Hamlet offers the observation that "a knavish speech sleeps in a foolish ear" (IV.ii.25).

In following the varying speech preferences of Hamlet—from "words of so sweet breath compos'd" to taciturnity, to "wild and whirling words," to passionate outbursts, to "words like daggers," and finally to silence—we may easily overlook the cunning with which Shakespeare has made Claudius an important part of Hamlet's world of words. Claudius is not only a symbol but a major participant in creating the verbal haze that Hamlet must cut through. Polonius, too, is of course a part; but his tedious precepts no longer serve very effectively to conceal the ugly truth. What Polonius thinks, he now directly utters, or he has come to believe what he utters. Unlike Hamlet, he does not attempt to conceal anything. When he learns of the supposed cause of Hamlet's madness, he immediately reveals that which,

> being kept close, might move
> More grief to hide than hate to utter love.
> (II.i.118)

With Claudius, however, it is entirely different. He, like Hamlet, must conceal his emotions; but he chooses to do so not by silence but by what he calls "speaking fair" (IV.i.36). Typically, his first thought upon hearing of Polonius' murder is that

> this vile deed
> We must, with all our majesty and skill,
> Both countenance and excuse.
>
> (IV.i.30)

And his concern when he decides to ship Hamlet away is to "bear all smooth and even," so that the sudden act will "seem / Deliberate pause" (IV.iii.7).

Countenancing and excusing his own "vile deed" occupies his considerable verbal talents during his first appearance on stage. At the same time he is disguising by fair words the hostility between him and his nephew. One need take only a few lines to appreciate the suavity and composure of his language in this difficult situation: " 'Tis sweet and commendable in your nature, Hamlet"; "Here in the cheer and comfort of our eye"; "Why, 'tis a loving and a fair reply"; "This gentle and unforc'd accord of Hamlet / Sits smiling to my heart." Hamlet's reaction to these genial expressions had been explicitly stated by Bassanio in *The Merchant of Venice:* "I like not fair terms and a villain's mind" (I.iii.180). But Hamlet's cold reception of his courteous phrase does not shake Claudius from the composure with which he conceals the evil that lies beneath his words. Even

when Laertes later rushes in upon him, and he is in
danger of being slaughtered, he hides magnificently behind the comfortable words that befit only a true king:

> Let him go, Gertrude; do not fear our person.
> There's such divinity doth hedge a king
> That treason can but peep to what it would,
> Acts little of his will.
>
> (IV.v.122)

As with Hamlet, it is only when Claudius is alone that
he allows emotion to shake his normal verbal control
of his terrible situation. Significantly, his first confession
of guilt, made in an aside, refers to the strain imposed
upon him by the necessity for making his speech conceal
his true nature:

> The harlot's cheek, beautied with plast'ring art,
> Is not more ugly to the thing that helps it
> Than is my deed to my most painted word.
> O heavy burden!
>
> (III.i.51)

A life of "painted words" is not easy even for an arch-
criminal, any more than a life of silence is easy for
Hamlet. In the orotund confidence of Claudius' speeches
we tend to overlook the strain. His ceremonious calm-
ness and words of goodwill obscure a struggle with full
and true expression. We tend, for example, to take at

face value his repeated expressions of eagerness to learn the true reason for Hamlet's "transformation," forgetting that such a revelation is the one thing he does not want.

But on the rare occasions when Claudius can break down and speak the truthful words about himself, the effect is overwhelming. This is of course particularly true of the prayer scene. Here he finds that in conversing with God, his "painted word" cannot help him:

> But, O, what form of prayer
> Can serve my turn? "Forgive me my foul murder"?
> That cannot be; since I am still possess'd
> Of those effects for which I did the murder.
>
> (III.iii.51)

In the heavenly court above,

> There is no shuffling, there the action lies
> In his true nature.
>
> (III.iii.61)

In brief, the word must be suited to the action. Finally, in this scene, he explicitly recognizes the futility of words unaccompanied by deeds:

> My words fly up, my thoughts remain below.
> Words without thoughts never to heaven go.
>
> (III.iii.97)

After this unnerving episode Claudius tries to per-
severe, at least on earth, with the proper words. But his
weakness has been fatally exposed to himself. That it
is now a part of his sense of defeat is hinted at in his
question to Laertes:

> What would you undertake,
> To show yourself your father's son in deed
> More than in words?
>
> (IV.vii.125)

Claudius cannot himself undertake the necessary steps
for his divine pardon; and the final sign of his holding
desperately onto calm, assured words occurs when he
sees his wife dying of the poison. He still will not
allow himself publicly to express his sense of the dis-
maying truth: "She swounds to see them bleed" (V.ii.
319). The grim revelation of his crime is made in no
public confession by Claudius; it is achieved, so appro-
priately for a play in which true feelings are wordless,
by events beyond the control of words.

> For murder, though it have no tongue, will speak
> With most miraculous organ.
>
> (II.ii.622)

It is interesting to try to account, by some criterion
other than theme and iteration, for Shakespeare's probable decision to make *Hamlet* a play that expresses both

the hero's and the villain's dilemmas in terms of speech and silence, painted words, and words like daggers. We usually think, and correctly so, of the Elizabethans as a people fascinated by words and savoring them to the full.[5] Roger Ascham had voiced more than a personal preference when he warned against slighting words in favor of substance: "Ye know not, what hurt ye do to learning, that care not for wordes, but for matter." [6]

But there came a countermovement for distrust of words and orators. Montaigne's influence—in part a temperamental one—was surely felt from his essay "Of the Vanitie of Words." In a comparison that resembles Claudius' likening of his painted words to painted women, he writes of orators and rhetoricians: "Those that make and paint women, commit not so foule a fault; for it is no great losse, though a man see them not, as they were naturally borne and unpainted: Whereas these professe to deceive and beguile, not our eies, but our judgement." [7] In this essay Montaigne also advances the theory that talking has always flourished most in corrupt commonwealths. Francis Bacon, who had in mind primarily the bad effect of words on learning, made

[5] One of the best modern accounts of this fascination is to be found in M. H. Mahood, *Shakespeare's Wordplay* (London, 1957), chap. i.

[6] *The Scholemaster* (1570), in *English Works of Roger Ascham,* ed. William Aldis Wright (Cambridge, England, 1904), p. 265.

[7] *The Essayes of Montaigne,* tr. John Florio (New York: Modern Library ed., n.d.), p. 263.

the famous dictum, echoed approvingly by Ben Jonson, that "the first distemper of learning [occurs] when men study words and not matter." [8] Words, he adds, "are but the images of matter; and except they have a life of reason and invention, to fall in love with them is all one as to fall in love with a picture." But Bacon's severe scholarly purpose, however influential it may have been in the development of English style, does not bear too directly upon the problems in *Hamlet,* even though in the play words do interfere with the quest for truth.

I find a closer approximation to *Hamlet* in Sir William Cornwallis, who wrote essays "Of Silence and Secrecie" and "Of Words." A quality similar to Hamlet's distrust of Polonius may be found in the statement: "Trueth hath fallen upon it so often and so commonly that it is a received precept not to trust a great talker with your secrets, for they have such a disease of wordes that like fier they will feede upon themselves if they want sustenance." [9] And there is a strong hint of the inadequacy of the word in relation to action, with a specific reference to "faire wordes," in the following:

I finde no man affecting actions more thoroughly then these people of faire wordes, which makes mee feare

[8] *The Advancement of Learning* (1605), Book I, in *Selected Writings of Francis Bacon,* ed. Hugh G. Dick (New York: Modern Library ed., 1955), p. 182.

[9] Essay. 47. "Of Wordes," in *Essayes,* by Sir William Cornwallis, the Younger, ed. Don Cameron Allen (Baltimore, 1946), p. 220.

these Ingrossers of speech are constituted of too much winde and ayre and want that solidity which is meete in the generation of this deere issue of ours—our actions, which never faile to resemble us more neerely then the children of our body.[10]

A still closer approximation to the play, with emphasis upon use of what the author calls "painted words" in a corrupt society, is to be found in Thomas Browne's preface to his translation (1570) of Joannes Sturmius' *A Ritch Storehouse or Threasurie for Nobility and Gentlemen.* Our time, he writes (sig. A 3),

> is so inclined, and as it were naturally bent to bestow upon barren and unhonest fruites, precious and golden names, that neyther can vertuous and prayse worthy workes enjoye their due and deserved tytles, being forestauled and defrauded by evill, neyther good deedes possesse their owne.

Now, he adds, men utter "painted wordes and smooth Rhetoricke, than matter good and precious, so that neyther the condicion of the cause, whether it be good or badde, can move them to saye eyther more or lesse." In another illuminating work, Fulke Greville's *Life of Sr. Philip Sidney,* there is added to the concept of painted words in a corrupt age that of a man (Sidney)

---

[10] Essay. 33. "Of Silence and Secrecie," *Essayes,* p. 115.

who, like Hamlet, learned to look beneath the word
to the action. "For to this active spirit of his, all depths
of the Devill proved but shallow fords; he piercing into
mens counsels, and ends, not by their words, oathes, or
complements, all barren in that age, but by fathoming
their hearts and powers, by their deeds. . . ." [11]

However, not all of the inspiration for depicting
Hamlet's oppressive world of words came from the
spirit of the age. Much of it could have been derived
from the feeling of depression that can come to any
professional writer who, like Shakespeare, has to deal
excessively with words and who increasingly in his works
passes from pleasure in them to a sense of their hollow-
ness. Even as early as *The Rape of Lucrece,* Shakespeare
had expressed the futility of words in moments of greatest need:

> Out, idle words, servants to shallow fools!
> Unprofitable sounds, weak arbitrators!
>
> (l. 1016)

In *Richard II* Shakespeare had effectively depicted the
contrast between the King's eloquence and the cold, hard
steel of Bolingbroke. The only true words are those
spoken painfully by the dying Gaunt:

[11] Fulke Greville, *The Life of the Renowned Sr. Philip Sidney.* In *Works,* ed. A. B. Grosart (Blackburn, England: The
Fuller Worthies' Library, 1870), IV, 39–40.

Where words are scarce they are seldom spent in vain,
For they breathe truth that breathe their words in
   pain.

(II.i.7)

This message may, incidentally, underlie the request
made of Horatio by the dying Hamlet:

And in this harsh world draw thy breath in pain
To tell my story.

(V.ii.358)

As he drew closer to the composition of *Hamlet*,
Shakespeare could well have become still more depressed
by the windy, unreal quality of words. In *1 Henry IV*
Falstaff does not, as Hamlet perhaps does, represent
an earnest projection of Shakespeare's own self into
a character; but Falstaff is credibly delineated, and no
reader can miss the realistic force of his disquisition
upon *honor* as a mere word: "What is honour? A word.
What is in that word honour? What is that honour?
Air; a trim reckoning!" (V.i.135). Still closer in date
and disillusionment to *Hamlet* is Troilus' realization
that Cressida's protestations of love are mere words:

Words, words, mere words, no matter from the heart;
Th' effect doth operate another way.
Go, wind, to wind, there turn and change together.

My love with words and errors still she feeds,
But edifies another with her deeds.

(V.iii.108)

In *Othello* a similar note is heard when Brabantio rejects the proffered verbal comfort of the Duke:

But words are words; I never yet did hear
That the bruis'd heart was pierced through the ear.

(I.iii.218)

King Lear, too, makes much of the disparity between
verbal protestation and actuality, as does *Timon of
Athens.*

Shakespeare, then, not only was living in an age increasingly distrustful of words and of protesting too
much; he also was perhaps growing weary of words as
an author and as an actor who strutted and fretted his
brief hour upon the stage. But though the growing distrust of words may be traced in his other plays, none
so perfectly dramatizes the feeling as does *Hamlet.*
Mainly it presents two families, reflecting the larger
society as a whole, that have tried to sustain themselves
upon the thin nourishment of "enforc'd breath." Hamlet himself, while indulging occasionally in the solace
of passionate or bitter words, succeeds ultimately in
laying bare the inner ugliness of a verbally decorous
exterior, and in so doing proves to the audience that

though "words," as Gertrude says, "be made of breath," breath must be made of life (III.iv.197). And although words can continue temporarily an almost independent existence, life will ultimately show through.

In his own spiritual pilgrimage, Hamlet moves from a world filled with words, words, words, to a place where the rest is silence. He did not, happily, know that generations of scholars would reverse the process.

INDEX

INDEX